PROCEDURES
FOR THE PHONOLOGICAL
ANALYSIS OF CHILDREN'S
LANGUAGE

PROCEDURES FOR THE PHONOLOGICAL ANALYSIS OF CHILDREN'S LANGUAGE, by David Ingram, Ph.D., is the second volume of the **Assessing Communicative Behavior Series**—Jon F. Miller, Ph.D., Professor and Section Head, Communicative Disorders, Waisman Center on Mental Retardation and Human Development, Series editor.

Published volumes:

ASSESSING LANGUAGE PRODUCTION IN CHILDREN:
  Experimental Procedures
  Jon F. Miller, Ph.D.

Volumes in preparation:

ASSESSING LANGUAGE COMPREHENSION IN CHILDREN:
  Experimental Procedures
  Jon F. Miller, Ph.D.

ASSESSING COGNITIVE PERFORMANCE:
  Piagetian Procedures
  Roberta Dihoff, Ph.D.

ASSESSING COMMUNICATIVE PERFORMANCE:
  Pragmatic Considerations

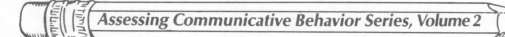

Assessing Communicative Behavior Series, Volume 2

PROCEDURES FOR THE PHONOLOGICAL ANALYSIS OF CHILDREN'S LANGUAGE

by

David Ingram, Ph.D.
Associate Professor
Department of Linguistics
University of British Columbia

UNIVERSITY PARK PRESS   Baltimore

UNIVERSITY PARK PRESS
International Publishers in Science, Medicine, and Education
300 North Charles Street
Baltimore, Maryland 21201

Typeset by University Park Press, Typesetting Division
Manufactured in the United States of America by
The Maple Press Company

Library of Congress Cataloging in Publication Data

Ingram, David, 1944-
Procedures for the phonological analysis of children's language.

(Assessing communicative behavior; v. 2)
Bibliography: p.
Includes index.
1. Language acquisition.   2.   Grammar, Comparative and general—
Phonology.   I.   Title.   II.   Series
P118.I45   401'.9   80-25371
ISBN 0-8391-1625-X

Contents

Foreword

The Assessing Communicative Behavior series presents clinical assessment procedures for evaluating multiple aspects of communication development including syntax, semantics, phonology, and pragmatics in both comprehension and production. The first volume, *Assessing Language Production in Children: Experimental Procedures,* contains procedures for assessing a child's syntactic, semantic, and pragmatic development over the first seven years. This second volume describes a series of detailed procedures for phonological analysis and completes the series coverage of productive language assessment.

With this volume, David Ingram has masterfully extended his landmark 1976 volume, *Phonological Disability in Children.* In 1976, Ingram presented several new concepts that have redirected the thrust of research and clinical practice in phonological disability. Two of these concepts, multiple levels of analysis and phonological processes, form the central theme of this volume.

Ingram presents here a set of related procedures that, taken together, provides a complete description of the developing phonological system. The four procedures, each presented in explicit detail, provide four levels of analysis of successive complexity. Each level of analysis is individually informative, beginning with the Phonetic Analysis, followed by the Analysis of Homonymy and the Substitution Analysis, and culminating with the Phonological Processes Analysis. These procedures provide us with the analytic tools to describe phonological development in successive levels of detail, each contributing to our understanding of the child's phonological system.

Here is a volume that we have long needed—one that makes explicit the relationship between articulatory proficiency and phonological processes. Ingram has provided us with a method for extending theory into practice. The procedures provide the means for describing normal patterns of phonological development and patterns of delayed development, which will ultimately lead to the explicit characterization of the range of variability in the acquisition of the sound system of English.

This volume contributes substantially to our ability to describe explicitly children's speech behavior, to judge its adequacy, and to direct the course of intervention. Ingram, in 1976, quoted Piaget: "...[the] theoretical fertility of a science is its capacity for practical application." With this volume, Ingram demonstrates the fertility of linguistic science and moves us toward the first step in developing a science of language disorders, that of clinical description.

Jon F. Miller
Series Editor

Preface

Since the appearance of my book in 1976, *Phonological Disability in Children*, I have had numerous discussions with its readers who constructively pointed out that it lacked one additional "chapter," one that would demonstrate explicitly how to do a phonological analysis in a step by step fashion. In response to these requests, I have attempted to put together the procedures I have developed over the years for this very purpose. This has been done in the hope of providing information that will be helpful to those practicing language clinicians who need to analyze children's phonological patterns on a regular basis, and also to my colleagues in the field who have been tackling, as I have, the various problems such analyses present. I hope this work sets a tone of explicitness that will characterize all of our future work.

For my knowledge of normal phonological development and the evolution of my thinking in the topic, I owe an enormous debt to the inspiring papers and conversations of several of my colleagues in the field, particularly Mary Louise Edwards, Carol Farwell, Charles Ferguson, John Locke, Marcy Macken, Lise Menn, and Carol Stoel-Gammon. I also would like to express my appreciation to those colleagues in the area of phonological disability, especially Arthur Compton, Barbara Hodson, Kim Oller, Elaine Paden, and Larry Shriberg, who have sharpened my understanding of the special problems of studying children with delayed development. I would like to extend a special acknowledgment to Larry Shriberg who more than anyone showed me the need for my "missing chapter," and to Jon F. Miller, who, as editor of the series, encouraged me throughout the development of the manuscript. The comparative study reported in Chapter 7 would not have been possible without the data collected and made available to me by Ricki Block, Debbie Bresler, Sally Jackson, Susan Payne, and Brendan Webster. Also, valuable input was received from Jane Fee, Barbara Hodson, Alan Kamhi, Harriet Klein, Larry Leonard, John Locke, Soumee Tse, and Fred Weiner who took time to read the preliminary manuscript and offer suggestions for revision. Last, I would like to offer a special thanks to Judith Johnston and Dee Tyack, to whom this book is dedicated. Their own work with and concern for linguistically handicapped children, both as language clinicians and colleagues in the investigation of language acquisition, has been a continuing inspiration to me. My own research and interest in language disorders in children have evolved directly from an admiration and respect of their commitment to this field of study, and I have benefited directly from their constant encouragement and support.

To   Judith Johnston
           Dorothy Tyack

PROCEDURES FOR THE PHONOLOGICAL ANALYSIS OF CHILDREN'S LANGUAGE

CHAPTER 1

Orientation

Glossary of Basic Terms

linguistics: the scientific study of language, with an emphasis on the structure of sound systems, words, sentences, and meanings, as well as on their historical development

phonetics: the study of the sounds of language in terms of their physical and articulatory characteristics

phonology: the branch of linguistics that studies how the sounds within a language function to signify meaning, that is, each language's sound pattern (phonological analysis)

1.1 PURPOSE

Since the advent of linguistics as a scientific discipline in the early 1900s, phonology has been one of its dominant areas of study. For almost as many years, linguists have attempted to apply their basic procedures to the study of children's developing sound patterns (e.g., Grammont, 1902). Although the range of this work has been formidable (c.f., references in Leopold, 1952; Slobin, 1972; Abrahamsen, 1977), the theoretical approaches diverse (c.f., review in Ferguson and Garnica, 1975), and the empirical findings extensive (c.f., review in Ingram, 1976, chapter 2), we still have only limited knowledge about the extent of variability between children, the difficulty of individual speech sounds, the origin of phonological contrasts (see below), and the relation between phonetic development and phonological development. One reason for this lack of knowledge is the fact that phonological analyses published to date are extremely diverse, and rarely rely on common procedures and definitions. Because of this diversity, comparison across studies is often difficult or impossible.

This point can be exemplified by looking at the general problem of determining the use of a particular speech sound. Can we say that [b] has been acquired when it is used in one, two, three or more words? Also, even if it is used a certain number of times, it may be that its use in these words varies with some other sound. Furthermore, there is the issue of comparing sounds to the adult model and the problem of determining when adult /b/ has been acquired, even if [b] is articulatorily produced. The criteria used in such decisions differ greatly among individual analysts and, therefore, the results also differ. Consequently, the field of child phonology is in need of a consistent set of procedures and criteria that may be used in phonological analysis to produce data and analyses that can be compared across studies.

While linguists are concerned with theoretical issues about the nature of rules and sound change in general, those persons working in the discipline of language disorders in children have more immediate interests, because they are confronted on a daily basis with children who are delayed in language and in need of language intervention. Because of this, virtually all of the normative data on phonological development come from scientists in this field (e.g., Templin, 1957). Here, the goal of analyses is to determine whether a child is delayed, and if so, the patterns that are most in need of remediation. Because norms require testing and quantification of data, the field has been marked by the development of tests and measures of acquisition.

In recent years, there has been an attempt to incorporate the analytic methods of linguistic analyses within the more quantitative approach of the language disorders field (c.f., review in Ingram, 1976, chapters 5, 6). There are, however, problems in doing this. First, the procedures that are suggested require measures and quantification that have not yet been done. Second, they need to be made explicit enough so that working clinicians can find them viable for use in situations in which time and linguistic training are necessarily restricted. For example, Ingram (1976, chapter 3) demonstrated a linguistic analysis of a set of data from a language-delayed child that may be helpful if read carefully enough, but it is unlikely that most clinicians would have the time for such detailed analyses even if they would be able to find the time to develop the analytic skills. Consequently, there is the need for an explicit set of analytic procedures that may be used by language clinicians to determine the prominent phonological patterns of a language-delayed child.

The purpose of this text, then, is to provide an explicit set of procedures that can be used in the phonological analysis of the speech of children, and that can be used: 1) with normal children for determining the "normal" patterns of phonological development in a way that allows comparison across investigators, and 2) with language-delayed children for determining the extent of delay, the patterns currently in use, and those aspects most immediately in need of remediation.

1.2 GOALS OF AN ANALYTIC PROCEDURE

Recently, investigators have begun to develop explicit "programs" of phonological analysis—notably, Weiner (1979); Shriberg and Kwiatkowski (1980); and Hodson (1980)—but these programs are restricted to use primarily with language-delayed children. These works are clinically oriented attempts to provide an instrument for clinicians to use in the evaluation of phonological processes (c.f., section 1.3 below) for purposes of remediation. The set of procedures presented in this book may be used for this purpose, but it also has a broader range of use

that can be seen by evaluating the possible goals of an analytic procedure.

The procedures described in the following chapters are meant to be complete, flexible, adaptive, cumulative, and normative.

For a program to be *complete,* it must look into all the diverse aspects of phonological acquisition. Given our incomplete knowledge in this field, this goal cannot be realistically achieved yet; however, it is possible to design a set of procedures that focuses on certain characteristics of a child's speech. The young child acquires a set of speech sounds, a phonetic inventory, that can be examined independently of the adult language. When comparing the child's language to the adult language, we can determine the pattern of substitutions that occurs. Last, we can examine the substitutions for general patterns (phonological processes) that occur. This work is not limited to any one of these aspects of phonological acquisition, rather, it attempts to look at all three in a manner consistent with the next four goals.

Besides being complete, an analysis program also needs to be *flexible* in terms of its data base. The phonological forms used for analysis may come from spontaneous speech samples, picture elicitation, or various methods used in articulation testing. If possible, the procedures recommended here should be used in conjunction with data from all these sources when making observations about the nature of a child's phonology. Such flexibility includes describing small samples as well as large ones, and recording variant pronunciations of the same word. The latter creates problems for many tests or programs that either ignore variant pronunciations or those that record only the first pronunciation of a particular word. The elimination of variable forms of pronunciation removes an important aspect of a child's data from consideration.

A third goal is that a program should be *adaptive* or capable of being adjusted to an individual child's problems. Often, programs, particularly behaviorist oriented ones, have a rigid set of steps that must be followed invariantly from beginning to end, regardless of the child's particular needs. One that is adaptive, however, will allow analysts to select the part that is most relevant to the child under observation. In such an approach, one may pick and choose, so to speak, and skip around as necessary.

A related aspect of adaptability regards the nature of the steps involved in the determination of a child's pattern. In one case, it can be quite difficult to see the reason behind a series of mechanical steps until the very last one has been reached. This can not only result in boredom for the analyst, but also in error in the recording of data. On the other hand, a program could be *cumulative,* in that the analyst's knowledge about the child's data is augmented through each step. In this case the analyst's enthusiasm will be triggered as knowledge accumulates after each step is completed, and, because the steps are self-contained, an analysis can be done over a period of time rather than in one long laborious session during which a pause would result in "losing your place." So, too, a cumulative program is one in which the reasons behind the various steps are explained to the potential user; understanding the means, not just the end, is an important part of the procedure.

Finally, an important goal of any set of analytic procedures is that it be *normative,* that is, endowed with explicit measures or counts that allow comparisons with data collected under the program by other persons. Some suggestions for the use of linguistic analysis, for example, are so unclear regarding definitions of rules and patterns that two independent users could come up with different analyses for the same set of data. Also, vagueness could result when the same person later changes his decisions about particular phenomena. If explicit measures are available, a program can become its own research instrument because data collected and analyzed by those using it accumulate over time.

The set of procedures for phonological analysis of children's languages, which is described in the following chapters, was designed to meet the five goals discussed above. First, it is more complete than other programs with which I am familiar, although other programs can always be augmented (c.f., discussion in section 1.3). It is flexible in that it can be applied to any kind or size of data, and it is adaptive to the extent that those who become familiar with it can pick and choose the particular analysis to be undertaken. I have attempted to make it as cumulative as possible, and to provide justification for the various steps within the text. Occasionally, decisions about the sequencing of particular steps were made arbitrarily or intuitively, as must happen from time to time. Such cases are pointed out. The program is also normative, and some research data have already been analyzed by this approach. (See Chapter 7.)

Summary of Goals

1. complete: covers different aspects of phonological development
2. flexible: can be any data, independent of manner of sampling, sample size, number of alternative pronunciations, etc.
3. adaptive: can be adjusted for analysis of particular features of individual children
4. cumulative: provides sets of analysis that are designed to provide new information on child at each step
5. normative: presents explicit criteria and measures that allow comparison of results across analysts.

1.3 FOUR KINDS OF PHONOLOGICAL ANALYSES

The procedures have been developed for four kinds of analyses: phonetic analysis, analysis of homonymy, substitution analysis, and phonological process analysis.

1.3.1 Phonetic Analysis

A phonetic analysis examines the speech sounds that a child produces, disregarding the adult model attempted. Such an analysis provides information on what the child can produce or articulate, and includes information on both segments (consonants and vowels) and syllables. Because of difficulties inherent in the transcription of vowels, the following procedures are limited to consonants and syllables, although they could be easily altered to include vowel data.

There are particular problems that an effective phonetic analysis needs to solve. One of these concerns the question of frequency. If the child produces two cases of word initial [p] and 25 of [b], should we say that the child produces both [p] [b], should we eliminate [p] because of lack of frequency, or should we include [p] but give [b] special status? You could even say that one production should be sufficient, but there are two particular problems with that: first, the fewer cases of a sound, the more likely it is that there might be a transcription error; and second, children tend to use with some frequency the sounds they can produce.

A question related to frequency is sample size. What size sample is necessary for us to conclude that it is adequate for claims about the phonetic inventory? A child with a small phonetic inventory will require fewer sounds to show this than a child with a larger one. Also, if one child produces two [b]s in a 50-word sample, and another produces two in a 100-word sample, do we conclude that each child has equal ability with [b]?

Another distributional problem concerns the number of times a sound may occur with different words or phonetic types. For example, suppose that a child uses initial [b] in five different words but all five are homonyms, so that there is only one phonetic form, let's say [bak]. In this case, the child may have a unit [bak] so that [b] is quite limited in its phonetic distribution. This is quite different from using [b] in five words, but having five different phonetic forms; compare, for example, [ba] [bu] [bik] [bæs] [bet]. We could decide to ignore words and deal only with the distribution of sounds in phonetic forms, but that also creates a problem. Consider, for example, two children who both have the phonetic forms [ba] [bak] [bæt]. We could say each has [b] three times, but suppose one child has used these as three alternant pronunciations of the word *bat* whereas the other has used them for three different words, *ball, back,* and *bat.* Do we want to say that the latter child has a wider use of [b] than the former child?

Another problem concerns the syllable position in which a sound occurs. Although some investigators group sounds, it is common to separate sounds into syllable initial, medial, and final position.[1] Should we, however, do this by word position or syllable position? For example, the word *turkey* is produced by a child as [kaka]. The adult word has three syllable positions, with [k] being syllable medial. For the child, however, if each syllable receives equal stress, which is quite likely (c.f., Allen and Hawkins, 1978), the second [k] is really a syllable initial position, but word medial. If we choose syllable, there is the further problem that few investigators transcribe stress patterns, and even fewer, syllable boundaries.

In the procedures for phonetic analysis described in Chapter 3, solutions are suggested for these problems, although they are tentative. Because transcription error is always a possibility, the inclusion of a minimum frequency criterion allows analysts to minimize this. Also, I decided that because children use preferred sounds, more frequent sounds have a special status that needs to be taken into account. Frequency measures are determined relative to sample size. The problems raised about the distribution of sounds in words versus phonetic forms are resolved by considering both kinds of distribution. In other words, for a sound to meet a minimum frequency criterion, it will need to occur in a certain number of words and phonetic forms. The decision about syllable versus word position was made on practical grounds. When looking at the child's phonetic inventory, placement of sounds is based on word position, except for certain simple cases of impossible clusters. (This is different in the case of substitution analysis; see below, where syllable position is used.) The result of these decisions is an explicit procedure that allows for the determination of a child's phonetic inventory for word initial, medial, and final position. When the procedure is completed, we can observe the number of sounds that meet the criterion and we can use this number as a gross measure of acquisition. Measures based on the child's phonetic inventory can be a phonological equivalent to MLU (mean length of utterance) as found in grammatical studies for placing children at gross levels of acquisition.

1.3.2 Analysis of Homonymy

Because phonetic types that are homonyms are marked in the phonetic analysis, it is possible to analyze the degree of homonymy in the child's data as a separate analysis. Ingram (1976) suggested that extensive homonymy may be a characteristic of delayed language in children. Although this is an empirical question still to be resolved, it is apparent that certain children, whether normal or delayed, demonstrate more homonymy than others (c.f., Vihman, 1979), and that this is an important aspect to determine for any individual child. Presumably, children with excessive homonymy will have greater difficulty in communicating, and may demonstrate other co-occurring patterns of acquisition.

The analysis of homonymy requires the development of a measure that may be used across children. The only measure currently available is that in Ingram (1974), which has been found to be problematic (c.f., Priestley, in press). There are at least two aspects of homonymy that need to be considered when developing a measure of its extent. Consider, for example, the data presented in Velten (1943) regarding the speech of his daughter Joan. This child is commonly cited (e.g., Priestley, in press) as one whose speech contained a great deal of homonymy. When examining the data, however, it can be shown that she had a great number of homonymous words for a small number of phonetic forms. The phonetic form [bat], for example, represented 12 words including *ball, bare, blue,* and *bowl* for the child when she was 22 months old. There were only three such phonetic forms, however, the other two being [bu] and [but]. The rest of the data showed little homonymy. Yet, another child may have a large proportion of its phonetic forms represent homonymous words. This requires keeping track of the extent of homonymy not only among words but also among phonetic forms. The analysis presented in Chapter 4, therefore, maintains a difference between these two kinds

---

[1]The term *medial* is used, in this book, to refer to the child's words. The term *ambisyllabic* (or *intervocalic*) refers to the adult's words.

of homonymy and proposes a new, separate measure for each.

1.3.3 Substitution Analysis

The most common form of phonological analysis of children's speech used over the years has been substitution analysis, that is, the determining of the child's substitutes for the target sounds of the adult language. Although at first glance this seems to be a simple matter of looking for mismatches between the child's speech and that of the adult, there are important decisions to be made and problems to be solved, as in the case of a phonetic analysis.

The most important one concerns the issue discussed above, word position versus syllable position. It is clear that children frequently use different substitutes for an adult sound depending on its position; therefore, it is necessary to discuss whether a sound is initial, medial, or final. For monosyllabic adult words there is no problem because we have only two possible consonant positions, initial and final, and there is no need to distinguish between syllable and word. Problems arise, however, when multisyllabic words are attempted.

First, let's consider a compound word such as *bathtub*. If we use word as our unit of analysis, we might be led to conclude that [θt] is a medial cluster of some kind, which obviously bears no relation to reality. If the child produces [bætʌ], we might claim that the child has [t] for adult medial /t/, a less obvious but just as erroneous conclusion. Compound words have a clear syllable boundary between the words that cause [θ] to be syllable final and [t] syllable initial. In these cases, however, we could decide that word is still the unit of analysis and that we treat compounds as two separate words.

More serious problems arise, however, with multisyllable noncompound words such as *napkin, paper, finger,* and *medicine*. If we use word as our unit of analysis, a word like *napkin* will have a medial cluster [pk], yet here, there is a syllable boundary that separates these two, with [p] being the last segment of the first syllable, and [k] the first segment of the second one. Data like these indicate that syllable rather than word should be chosen as our unit of analysis for the determination of segment position. Once we do this, however, other problems arise. Because syllables only have beginnings and ends, such a decision means that there is no longer a medial position. If so, then what do we do with words like *paper* and *finger*? Phonetically speaking, at least, it is clear that we do not say [peɪ.pər] or [peɪp.ər] (here, . indicates a clear syllable boundary), nor [fiŋ.gər] or [fiŋg.ər]. In these cases, the word internal segments

are ambisyllabic in the sense that they function both to end one syllable and to begin another. The decision to use syllables necessitates the development of explicit criteria for the placement of syllable boundaries and consequently ways to separate ambisyllabic consonants from initial and final ones.

In substitution analysis, decisions also need to be made about the frequency of different kinds of substitutes. Consider, for example, a child who uses [g] as a substitute for adult /k/ in the words *car* [ga], *cat* [gæ], and *cake* [gek], but uses [t] in *cup* [tʌ]. We can say that [g] occurs 75% of the time and [t], 25%. Is this the case, however, with the child who has the speech forms *car* [ga] [gæ] and *cat* [gæ] [tæ]? If we count substitutes in different phonetic types, we claim that these two children are the same. If, however, we use word as the criterion, then the latter child shows a use of [t] in 50% of the words.

A related problem arises in regard to decisions about correct production of adult words. Suppose we have the following data from a child on the production of adult /t/: *top* [ta], *toe* [to], *teeth* [tif], and *two* [tsu] [du] [gu] [bu]. If we used phonetic forms as our unit of analysis, then /t/ is correct only three out of seven times whereas if we used word, then three out of four show correct production. When we allow data to include more than one production of a word, problems like these begin to occur and they require decisions for analysis.

The response of other investigators to problems like these is often one of avoidance. In the case of segment position, usually initial, medial, and final positions are presented with little description of how these are determined. The difficulties with frequency are circumvented by either testing for any one production of a test sound (e.g., Templin, 1957) or using only one production of a word (e.g., Shriberg and Kwiatkowski, 1980). Data from acquisitions that take variable production into account, however (c.f., Ingram et al., in press), show that acquisition is gradual and that variation is an important aspect of development.

A last point concerns the extent to which substitutions occur throughout a child's phonology. Unfortunately, this is a question that has been poorly researched, so I can only offer some impressions here. Recall that a child either produces a sound correctly, omits it, or else he or she uses a substitute some of the time. It seems that some children early in development produce sounds correctly, or else they avoid words that have difficult sounds. In these cases, the children would actually show few substitution patterns in their speech. Others, however, seem to have widespread substitutions throughout their system.

(These, in fact, are the children who researchers constantly seek because through them, much can be learned about strategies of phonological acquisition.) Also, individual children may show different abilities for different syllable positions (c.f., Renfrew, 1966; Ingram, 1979). For example, a child may have accurate production of initial segments, but he or she may do quite poorly on final ones. If future research indicates that such differences between children exist, then the analysis of an individual child's substitutions will need to address those differences.

The procedures in Chapter 5 suggest how to analyze a child's substitutions by taking these factors into account. In regard to segment position, the syllable is chosen as the most revealing unit of analysis. Guidelines are presented that show how syllable boundaries are placed in adult words and how ambisyllable segments can be distinguished from initial and final ones. Also in the procedures, decisions about frequency, which place primary importance on the word rather than phonetic types (although the latter are also considered), are made. Last, the chapter proposes a tentative measure for the overall extent to which a child uses substitutions. This measure may be used to determine whether the child uses more substitutes in one position than another, and also whether a child substitutes much at all. It can also be used as a means of deciding whether a phonological process analysis of the kind discussed below needs to be undertaken. A child with few substitutes will be one who is using few phonological processes.

1.3.4 Phonological Process Analysis

Phonological processes refer to kinds of changes, which apply to classes of sounds, not just individual sounds, that children make in simplifying adult speech. For example, if the child replaces an adult /s/ with a [t], it is also possible that other fricative sounds may, in turn, be changed into corresponding stop consonants. These changes can be grouped together as a general process of Stopping (c.f., Ingram, 1976, for a review of these). The postulation of phonological processes instead of individual substitutions has the advantage of bringing related sound changes together and provides a more explanatory description of development.

An analysis of a child's speech for phonological processes logically follows a substitution analysis because it is an attempt to provide a broader explanation of what, at first glance, may seem to be unrelated changes. The interest in phonological processes in recent years, stemming from Stampe's (1969) original work, has led to analyses of both normal and delayed speech (c.f., Ingram, 1976, for a review of this literature) and also to recent programs (e.g., Shriberg and Kwiatkowski, 1980) and assessment procedures (e.g., Weiner, 1979) for use with language-delayed children.

Because it is a new domain of phonological analyses, the study of the processes used by children requires careful research, particularly in terms of the nature and diversity of processes. Even so, we know enough about general features of the most common processes to develop means for their analysis; however, it is necessary to be cautious in applying the analysis and in constructing careful criteria for the determination of phonological processes.

One decision that needs to be considered in developing a set of procedures for phonological process analysis is whether processes are assumed to be an *open* or *closed* set. In reality, we do not know the full range of possible processes, therefore, as far as research is concerned, they are an open set. This is true even though, on a theoretical level, we hope to be capable, eventually, of providing a complete list, or closed set, of possible processes. The assumption that the number of processes is open-ended was made in Ingram (1976) in which process analysis was presented as a combination of one's knowledge of common processes and one's creative ability to analyze linguistic data for other less obvious or less common processes. Although the approach is viable for those with training in linguistic analyses, it may be unfeasible for many analysts working in a clinic, where linguistic background often is limited and time for analysis restricted. For these reasons as well as others, Shriberg and Kwiatkowski (1980) suggested that an analysis should focus on a closed set of basic processes.

A more serious situation arises when we attempt to decide how to define a process. Consider, for example, the process of Stopping, in which the child changes adult fricative sounds into stops. Suppose we have a child who changes all fricatives into corresponding stops, for example, f ⟶ p, s ⟶ t, ʃ ⟶ t or k. We can say that Stopping has occurred. Another child, however, may produce /f/ correctly, but change /s/ to [t] 50% of the time, and /ʃ/ to [t] all of the time. We can say that Stopping is less frequent now, yet we could also discuss three processes, /s/ Stopping, /f/ Stopping, and /ʃ/ Stopping, because all these show different patterns. If we do this (not an unreasonable decision), then we are in the awkward situation of claiming that the child with the more advanced language has more simplifying processes than the less advanced child. This is a major problem because all processes will show varying degrees of application from speech sound to speech sound, thus creating definitional problems of this kind. So too, any program of analysis, to be insightful, will need to be capable of showing the individual patterns of the processes.

A related problem occurs regarding decisions about how to measure processes. Suppose that the child has /f/ correct (five instances), /s/ → [t] (three instances) and /s/ correct (five instances), and /ʃ/ → [t] (two instances). If we add these up, Stopping has occurred only in five out of 15 potential cases for a 33% rate of occurrence. Another child may have /f/ → [p] (one instance) and /f/ correct (two instances), /s/ → [t] (one instance) and /s/ correct (two instances), and /ʃ/ → [t] (one instance) and /ʃ/ correct (two instances). This child also has a 33% rate of occurrence of stopping, but it would obviously be misleading to say that the children use stopping in the same ways. Variations like this will occur across syllable position as well as across sounds.

The procedures in Chapter 6 suggest how to do a fairly complete phonological process analysis in a way that resolves some of these dilemmas. First, a decision as to whether a complete analysis is warranted must be made. An analysis of the child's substitutions will make it possible to determine in advance the dominant processes. Then, a selected analysis may be done. The chapter discusses ways to outline a selective analysis. For children with widespread substitutions, however, a complete analysis will probably be necessary. For this purpose, in Chapter 6, the 27 dominant processes evident in the speech of delayed children are explicitly described and are analyzed quantitatively. These analyses are given first for individual sounds and syllable positions, and data are only grouped under general patterns if similar rates of occurrence exist. Although it seems that a closed set of processes are selected, the analysis also provides for information to be entered on other less frequent processes. The analysis proceeds until all the substitutions in the child's speech have been explained. The final data are then summarized and those processes that occur never, infrequently, frequently, and always, are noted.

1.3.5 Summary of Analyses

As mentioned in section 1.2, the procedures outlined in this book are as complete as possible, given what we currently know about phonological acquisition and what is possible to describe with an explicit series of steps. The analyses to be described may be summarized as follows, given the decisions made regarding the issues discussed above:

Phonetic Analysis The determination of the child's phonetic inventory for word initial, word medial, and word final positions, and a numerical count that can be used as a gross measure of development.

Analysis of Homonymy The establishment of the extent of homonymy in a child's speech by the use of a measure that gives the proportion of a) homonymous words and b) homonymous phonetic forms.

Substitution Analysis The recording of the substitutions the child uses for adult segments that are syllable initial, syllable final, and ambisyllabic, and also a measure of the extent of substitutions.

Phonological Process Analysis The calculation of the percentage of occurrence of 27 common phonological processes, as well as those that are less frequent, and division into those that occur never, sometimes, frequently, and always.

1.4 FORMS FOR PHONOLOGICAL ANALYSIS

A set of forms has been designed for the four kinds of analysis discussed in section 1.3. These forms provide a complete record of the child's data, and they can be placed on file and compared to later data to determine developmental advances and possible effects of intervention. They are not divided into separate forms for each individual analysis, instead they represent different ways to organize phonological data. In the rest of this section the structure and purpose of these forms are briefly introduced; the following chapters and appendices provide detailed examples and demonstrations of their use.

The procedures for phonological analysis make use of eight forms, which are labeled as follows (see Appendix A for sample copies of each of these):

1. Lexicon Sheet
2. Consonant Inventory Sheet—Lexical Types
3. Consonant Inventory Sheet—Phonetic Forms
4. Item and Replica Sheet
5. Child Syllable Sheet
6. Homonymy Sheet
7. Phonological Processes Sheet
8. Summary Sheet

The Lexicon Sheet consists of blank rows and columns and is designed to record the child's phonological data in a way that allows for quick retrieval of the child's speech forms. On it, the child's words are placed in alphabetical order, with variant pronunciations, if any, indicated. The advantage of this form over other commonly used types, such as index cards, is that it allows for reduction of data onto one or two pages—a single Lexicon Sheet can record more than 100 words. For example, the data given on Lexicon Sheet 3, in Chapter 3, for the child referred to as R shows 90 words alphabetically recorded on a single page. If data are taken from spontaneous samples, the number of utterances can be indicated on the original transcript from which the word has been taken. If a standardized articulation test is used, then the adult words can be entered in advance and individual children's productions can be added as they are tested.

The Consonant Inventory Sheets contain boxes that are used for grouping all of the English consonants. The one labeled *Phonetic Forms* is used in the Phonetic Analysis, and the one labeled *Lexical Types* is used in the Substitution Analysis. In the Phonetic Analysis, the Consonant Inventory Sheets record the occurrence of the consonants produced by the child, with separate ones used for word initial, word medial, and word final position, respectively. Appendices C.2 to C.4 show the data for R recorded on these forms. They clearly show the child's frequent use of a limited number of sounds in each word position. The forms are used slightly differently in the Substitution Analysis. In this case, the adult words the child has attempted are entered for each consonant, and a separate form is used for syllable initial, syllable final, and ambisyllabic segments. Then, next to each word, the sound the child produces for the adult target sound is entered. If the child said [ga] for dog, for example, this would be entered as

(with the "g" recorded in red ink for ease of analysis later) in the box marked with *d* on the page where syllable initial consonants are entered. The data from R, Appendices E.3 to E.5, also provide an example of how this is done. These three Consonant Inventory sheets—one each for word initial, ambisyllabic, and final positions—provide a complete record of all of the child's substitutions.

The Item and Replica Sheet consists of six box diagrams that are used for summarizing the data from the Consonant Inventory Sheets. Each of these diagrams is a chart of English consonants, a descriptive method adapted from Ferguson (1968). (See also Klein, 1977, for an effective use of Ferguson's method of analysis.) The three diagrams on the left of the page represent the initial, medial, and final consonants that the child produces. Here, the frequency of each sound in the child's phonetic inven-

tory is entered, and those that are frequent (as determined by a criterion discussed in Chapter 3) are circled. The three diagrams on the right of the page represent syllable initial, syllable final, and ambisyllabic segments. They are blank and are to be filled with the child's productions for the target adult sounds in the corresponding boxes in the diagram to the left. Below is an example of the top part of an Item and Replica Sheet and how this works.

word initial segments		syllable initial consonants	
m 1	n 1	b (7)	d (6)

On the left, the entry of *1* next to *m* and *n* means that the child produced one phonetic type that began with an [m] and one that began with [n]. Such low frequencies suggest an inability to produce nasal sounds, but it also may mean that the child did not produce many adult words that have initial nasals. The diagram on the right, however, shows that the child has a difficulty with nasals, because the child's major substitute for adult /m/ was [b] (seven instances), and for adult /n/ it was [d] (six instances). The Item and Replica Sheet allows you to place on a single page a summary of the child's phonetic inventories in terms of what the child both can and cannot produce, and also a summary of the more frequent substitutions.

The Child Syllable Sheet consists of a range of possible syllable shapes on one axis and word initial segments on the other. Here, the frequency of the syllables used by the child can be recorded by entering the number of each type, as calculated from the Consonant Inventory Sheet—Phonetic Forms, that shows the child's word initial segments. These data are part of the Phonetic Analysis, which is used to study not only the child's use of segments but also use of syllables. They indicate whether the child uses multisyllabic words and they indicate preferred syllable shapes such as CV, CVC, where C=consonant and V=vowel.

The child's use of homonyms is shown on the Homonymy Sheet. This form is used to record the homonymous forms that the child uses (e.g., [bat], and the homonymous lexical types each represents, e.g., *back*, *box*). Also, the bottom of the form contains simple formulas for the calculation of specific measures of homonymy. Two of these are the Ratio of Homonymous Forms and the Ratio of Homonymous Types, which state the ratio of nonhomonymous to homonymous forms and types, respectively. Also, there are two proportions of homonymy calculated, and these are also separate for forms and types.

The most detailed form is the Phonological Processes Sheet, which is used for the recording of the frequency of phonological processes. This form gives a breakdown of the child's use of the major phonological processes and calculates a proportion of occurrence for each segment and syllable position where a process could potentially apply. The processes are divided into the three major groups: Syllable Structure Processes, Substitution Processes, and Assimilation Processes. The form also contains space for entering the less common processes that an individual child may use.

The last form is the Summary Sheet, which encapsulates the major results of all four analyses on a single page. The form is used to record the child's phonetic inventory, from the Phonetic Analysis, for word initial, medial, and final positions, along with the measures of Total Number of Sounds and the Articulation Score. Also, the number of different types of syllable structure are entered on this form. The calculation of the two measures of homonymy, that is, the proportion of homonymous forms and homonymous words, are entered on the Summary Sheet. From the Substitution Analysis, a summary of the most frequent substitutions is entered and the calculation of proportion of substitutes (or mismatches) is made. Also, this form contains a summary of the child's phonological processes in which the processes are shown according to whether they occur never, sometimes, frequently, and always.

The use of the six forms for each of the four kinds of analysis can be summarized as follows:

Phonetic Analysis

Lexicon Sheet(s)
Consonant Inventory Sheets—Phonetic Forms
Child Syllable Sheet
Item and Replica Sheet
Summary Sheet

Analysis of Homonymy

Lexicon Sheet(s)
Consonant Inventory Sheets—Lexical Types
  (word initial forms from Phonetic Analysis)
Homonymy Sheet
Summary Sheet

Substitution Analysis

Lexicon Sheet(s)
Consonant Inventory Sheets—Lexical Types (3)
Item and Replica Sheet
Summary Sheet

Phonological Process Analysis

Consonant Inventory Sheets—Lexical Types (3)
  (from Substitution Analysis)
Phonological Processes Sheet
Summary Sheet

This summary can be used in selecting forms for an individual analysis. As stated in section 1.2, any one of these analyses can be done separately. There is some overlap in the case of the Analysis of Homonymy in that the procedure for recording the phonetic forms of the child according to their initial segments needs to be done, and this is normally part of the Phonetic Analysis. The Phonological Process Analysis is assumed to follow the Substitution Analysis and to make use of its recording of substitutions, but it could be done without doing a Substitution Analysis. This alternative is described in Chapter 6.

For a complete phonological analysis, doing all four analyses, all eight forms will be used. The forms should be kept in the following order:

1. Summary Sheet
2. Item and Replica Sheet
3. Phonological Processes Sheet
4. Three Consonant Inventory Sheets—Lexical Types (used in Substitution Analysis)
5. Homonymy Sheet
6. Three Consonant Inventory Sheets—Phonetic Forms (used in Phonetic Analysis)
7. Child Syllable Sheet
8. Lexicon Sheet(s)

1.5 FORMAT OF DESCRIPTION

The chapters that discuss and present the four kinds of phonological analyses (Chapters 3 to 6) are organized in the same manner to facilitate reading and understanding and to allow for easy retrieval of information during later use of the procedures. Each chapter begins with a Glossary of Basic Terms. In some instances, the definitions will already be familiar to the reader; however, the definitions are provided so that readers can review and confirm the way in which they are used in this book. In other cases, general terms such as phonetic form are used in a very specific and new way, which needs to be explained. The procedure contains just a few of these expressions that have been operationalized for analytic purposes.

Next, there is a brief statement of the goals of the analysis, followed by a list of the forms to be used. Some of this information is mentioned in sections 1.3 and 1.4 but is included again to permit each analysis chapter to be self-contained. The steps to be followed for each analysis are presented in two parts. First, a brief summary of the steps is given in a clearly identified box diagram. These are numbered sequentially in the text and labeled *Summary Box.* This is done to introduce the steps and also to provide a summary that may be referred to after users become familiar with the procedure. This summary is followed by a detailed set of instructions for these steps in which criteria are defined and procedures are elaborated on. When necessary, the instructions include some brief remarks about the rationale behind some of these decisions. Alternatives, when they exist, also are pointed out.

The last part of each chapter is devoted to a demonstration of the implementation of the procedures. This is done by first presenting and analyzing data on a child and discussing how the steps were followed. Next, a second set of data is given along with sample pages, and the reader is asked to try to do an analysis. The author's own analysis of the second set of data is contained in the appendices, along with a brief discussion. When the various analysis forms are presented for demonstration, they are labeled *Sample Analysis* and are numbered sequentially in the text. Those used in the sections for practice by the reader are labeled *Practice Pages.* Nontextual information is thereby presented in five distinct formats: 1) Glossary of Basic Terms, 2) Tables, 3) Summary Boxes, 4) Sample Analyses, and 5) Practice Pages.

Summary of Format (Chapters 2-6)

> Glossary of Basic Terms
> Goals of Analysis
> Forms Used
> Summary of Analytic Steps
> Detailed Instruction
> Sample Analysis
> Practice

CHAPTER 2

The Organization of Data

Glossary of Basic Terms

lexicon: a listing of the child's words in alphabetical order according to the adult spelling of the words

broad phonetic transcription: the representation of the child's word in a phonetic alphabet, such as the International Phonetic Alphabet (IPA), without the use of diacritics

narrow phonetic transcription: a detailed representation of a child's word in a phonetic notation that includes diacritics to show aspiration, vowel length, release of consonants, etc.

2.1 GOALS OF DATA ELICITATION, TRANSCRIPTION, AND ORGANIZATION

The elicitation of the child's speech
The phonetic transcription of the data
The organization of the lexicon

2.2 FORMS USED

Lexicon Sheet(s) for the organization of the lexicon

2.3 SUMMARY OF STEPS

Summary Box 1. Steps in the Organization of Data

1. *Elicitation of speech from the child*—through the use of either a speech sample, phonological diary, or articulation test
2. *Phonetic transcription of the data*—into as narrow a transcription as possible
3. *Organization of the lexicon*—data are placed in alphabetical order onto the Lexicon Sheet, and reduced to a broad phonetic transcription

2.4 DISCUSSION OF PROCEDURES

2.4.1 The Elicitation of Phonological Data

Obviously, the first step in any phonological analysis is collection of the data. Because one of the goals of the procedures presented in this book is that they be suitable for the analysis of data that is collected in a variety of ways (c.f., section 1.2, discussion of a flexible program), a predetermined set of instructions for data collection is not given. (Also, this topic is discussed in some detail in Ingram (1976, chapter 4).) Instead, I will briefly discuss three alternative ways in which data may be obtained for analysis. These are:

1. Spontaneous language sample
2. Phonological diary
3. Elicitation and testing

The choice of one method over the other is left to the circumstances and preferences of the analyst.

A *spontaneous language sample* is simply a sample of the child's speech obtained under naturalistic circumstances such as play or activities of normal family life. Such samples are usually taken for the purpose of grammatical analysis, but they may also be used for phonological analysis. If a language sample is available for a child, it is possible to use it for obtaining phonological data, but there are certain disadvantages that need to be recognized. First, these samples are rarely phonetically transcribed, therefore, re-listening to the original audio tape may be required. More problematic, however, is the fact that these samples do not always provide a wide sampling of the child's vocabulary. Often, even a long language sample produces a meager phonological sample with no instances of attempts at several adult sounds. The advantages are that the words collected are produced without prompting and they occur in context.

A *phonological diary* is a diary that is compiled over a period of days during which the analyst writes down in phonetic form the child's productions of adult words. This is the method often used by parents who are linguists because it enables the collection of a wide range of words that may constitute a complete record of all the child's words. A pad is kept handy on which the observer dates each word entered. Although this method produces a wider corpus of data, it does have certain disadvantages. For one, the method does not lend itself to careful recording of the rate of variable pronunciation of individual words. Alternate productions may be recorded, but usually only with impressionistic descriptions such as "most frequent," and "new production." Second, the method requires on-site transcription, which does not allow the analyst to play back the word to check for accuracy. However, children often repeat their words, so the more frequent forms of words are usually recorded accurately. In terms of time, however, it can be a more efficient method than general language sampling for obtaining a complete phonological sample.

The third and most frequently used method is *elicitation and testing*, a technique that involves manipulating the environment in order to get the child to produce specific words. This can be done quite unobtrusively by, for example, showing the child a preselected set of toys or pictures, or, through more controlled methods by having the child take a standardized articulation test that includes imitation. The advantages of a test are that it provides words for a wide range of sounds and also, it usually does not take too much time to administer. The major disadvantage is that it does not usually yield a wide range of data.

The selection of one method over another, as is stated above, is left to individual preferences. In nor-

mal language studies, often analysts have little choice if a range of data is desired. For example, published data often consist of phonological diaries, although most children recently studied have audio records of spontaneous samples (e.g., Brown, 1973). Other data report only the results from articulation tests (e.g., Templin, 1957). All three methods are well suited for clinical use. The collection of a language sample could be incorporated into the standard procedures that take place when a child enters therapy. This sampling could include play with toys the names of which include a variety of speech sounds. The sample could be used for grammatical and phonological purposes, and could become a record for future comparisons. Phonological diaries are not usually used in a clinical setting, yet they could be included in a way that could benefit both parents and clinicians. The parents could be shown how to do a broad phonetic transcription and then they could be asked to collect a phonological diary over a one-week period. The clinician could then go over the diary with the parents to check for errors. This would give the clinician more time to concentrate on the analysis of data. Articulation tests, which are widely utilized, could also be used in combination with one of the other methods, particularly for cases in which particular sounds need to be observed in more detail.

2.4.2 Phonetic Transcription

Data should always be transcribed in as narrow a phonetic transcription as possible; whether this can be done, however, depends on the extent of the analyst's phonetic training, the quality of the audio recording (if one is used), and the availability of other transcribers. It is extremely helpful to have someone check the transcriptions for questionable aspects. This recommendation, however, refers to the transcription of data for a permanent record. (As is discussed in section 2.4.3, it is recommended that only a broad transcription be entered as in the Lexicon Sheet and be used in the general analysis.)

A broad transcription is used here to mean a transcription that uses phonetic symbols without the inclusion of diacritics. All data should at least be transcribed minimally into a broad phonetic transcription. Tables 1 and 2 contain phonetic symbols that are used for the broad transcriptions that occur in this manual. Most of these symbols are from the International Phonetic Alphabet as adapted by Ladefoged (1975). Commonly used alternant symbols are shown in parentheses.

A narrow transcription is defined here as one that includes a variety of diacritics to add phonetic detail. For example, stop consonants can be transcribed to show whether they are aspirated ([pº]), partially voiced ([b̬]), or unreleased ([p°]). Vowels may be marked for nasality ([ã]) and length ([a:]). Some diacritics that may be found in narrow transcriptions are indicated at the bottom of Tables 1 and 2.

The forms used for the permanent record of the child's data depend on the method of elicitation. If a language sample is used, the data will be entered, presumably, in a notebook of some kind. Discussion can be found in Bloom and Lahey (1978) on how to take language samples and place them into a particular format. Ingram (in preparation) describes a method of language sampling that requires the use of phonetic transcription and adapts suggestions contained in Scollon (1976). These are provided in Summary Box 2. The sample can be placed in any notebook, so, no forms are supplied in this manual for that purpose. An example of how such a recording of a language sample will look is in sections 2.5 and 2.6.

Summary Box 2.   Suggested Steps in the Transcription of a Language Sample

1. Divide each page in half, placing the child's utterances on the left side, and the adult utterances on the right.
2. First listening to tape: transcribe child's utterance into a broad phonetic transcription (in black ink). Write adult utterances in standard adult orthography.
3. Second listening: add phonetic detail and changes to first transcriptions of child's utterances (in blue ink). They can be above previous transcription if necessary, e.g.,

$$[\overset{g}{d\circ}]$$

    where [g] is in blue and indicates that [g] and not [d] was heard at second listening.
4. Third listening: add contextual notes on what is taking place in sample where space is available to the right of the child's utterance (in green ink). Add morpheme by morpheme transliterations of the child's utterances to the left of the phonetic transcription (in red ink). Also, number all of the child's utterances for reference purposes (in red ink). Place uncertain transliterations in angle brackets < >, and unknown stretches in blank phonetic brackets. For example:

"go house" (red ink)	7.	gɔ haʊ (black ink)	(child puts doll into doll house) (green ink)
" <away> house"	8.	awe haʊ	(child puts doll behind house)
"[ ] car"	9.	dubʌ ka	(child picks up car)

If a phonological diary is used, the data can be kept in the pocket notebook in which they are originally recorded. The important point is to make sure that the data of utterances is recorded, and that notes are included to indicate whether entries are typical or novel productions. If an articulation test is used, the forms for the recording of the data will be part of the test so that no additional forms are required for that method. If the test is audiorecorded, the transcription can be based on multiple listenings and can contain as much phonetic detail as possible.

2.4.3 The Organization of the Lexicon

Once data are elicited and transcribed, they are then ready to be reduced and organized in a way that will allow for quick retrieval for purposes of analysis. This can be done by placing the child's words into alphabetical order on one or two condensed pages. The Lexicon Sheet has been designed for this purpose.

Step 1. **Number all utterances in the record of the child's speech if this has not yet been done.**

(This is done so that the permanent record can be checked later if necessary.)

Step 2. **Label 26 index cards each with a different letter of the alphabet**

On the cards, enter the words attempted by the child according to their first letter and the number of the utterance in which they occur. For example:

A	WORDS	UTTERANCE NUMBERS
	apple	3, 6, 17, 25
	ask	12

Do not worry about keeping the words in alphabetical order on the individual cards, but put them in the order in which they first appear in the sample.
Note: List contractions as a single word, for example, can't, I'll. If both contracted and uncontracted forms occur, for example, there and there's, list each separately. Also, if cards are not available, or if the sample is small, a page or two of any paper may be used.

Step 3. **Number the words within each card (or letter heading) according to their proper alphabetical order, to the left of the words**

B	WORDS	UTTERANCE NUMBERS
3	boat	12, 17
1	bat	6
2	big	13, 27
4	break	12, 18

This numbering is used for placing the words in alphabetical order on the Lexicon Sheet.

Table 1. Phonetic symbols of a range of possible consonant sounds that may be used in making a broad phonetic transcription[a]

Manner of articulation	Place of articulation					
	Labial	Dental/ alveolar	Palato- alveolar	Palatal	Velar	Glottal
Stops	p, b	t, d		c, ɟ	k, g	ʔ
Fricatives[b]	f, v	θ, ð	ʃ (š), ʒ (ž)		x, ɣ	h
central		s, z				
lateral		ɬ				
Affricates		ts, dz	tʃ (č) dʒ (ɣ)			
Nasals	m	n		ɲ (ɲ̈)	ŋ	
Approximants						
lateral		l				
central	(w)	r		j(y)	w	
tap		ɾ				

[a]Alternative symbols are placed in parentheses. Sounds next to each other separated by a comma are voiceless and voiced sounds, respectively.

[b]The lateral voiceless fricative [ɬ] is combined in the fricative class; some possible diacritics are as follows (where C=consonant sound): aspiration [Cʰ]; partially voiced [C̥]; retroflexed [C̣]; dentalized [C̪]; unreleased [C°]; velarized [C̴], as in [ɬ].

Step 4. **Enter the words attempted by the child and the child's production of them on the Lexicon Sheet**

This is done in alphabetical order by putting the first adult form of the word onto the far left column of the Lexicon Sheet, and then using the utterance numbers on the cards to look up the child's productions. The child's productions are then placed to the right of the adult word. When the first two columns are filled, go on to the next two columns in the same way. There are four pairs of columns on the Lexicon Sheet for this purpose, for a total of 124 spaces for the child's productions. Entries of the child's productions should be done as follows:

1. If only one production of a word occurs, enter as in this example:

    "dog" [dɔ]

2. If several productions of a word occur, but they have the same phonetic form, enter the form once then show the number of times it occurs, for example:

    "cat" [kæ] (6x)

Table 2. Phonetic symbols for vowels[a]

	Front	Central	Back
High			
tense	i		u
lax	ɪ		ʊ (ʊ)
Mid			
tense	e (eɪ)		o (oʊ)
lax	ɛ	ə	ɔ
Low	æ	ʌ	ɑ (a)
Diphthongs	[aʊ] "house"	[ɔɪ] "boy"	

[a]Some possible diacritics are as follows (where V=vowel): long [V:] or [V̄]; nasalized [Ṽ].

3. If a word is pronounced in more than one way, enter each way separately and show how often each occurs, for example:

    "fish" [fɪ] (3x)
    [pɪs] (2x)

4. If some of the words are spontaneous and others are imitations, distinguish the imitations by entering them in red ink.

5. Only enter child's productions onto the Lexicon Sheet in a broad phonetic transcription. If record is in narrow transcription, leave off the diacritics when entering productions onto Lexicon Sheet. This is done to eliminate the risks of errors in the transcription because narrow transcription requires more careful judgments about production. Also, keep glottal stops only when they occur as single consonants between vowels or at the end of words or syllables, but not when in clusters within a syllable; for example, narrow [ʔo], [oʔo], [oʔ] and [doʔk] become [o], [oʔo], [oʔ] and [dok], respectively, in a broad transcription.

6. Indicate words that occur in sentences by placing dashes around the phonetic types, for example, [-da] indicates a word preceded it whereas [da-] means that it is the first word of an utterance. This information may be important later when, for example, certain substitutions may only appear in phonetic types that occur sentence internally. A check with the original data may reveal a neighboring sound that causes the substitution.

2.5 EXAMPLE OF A LANGUAGE SAMPLE AND ITS LEXICON

Table 3 contains 25 utterances from a language sample collected from a young normal child, D, age 2;0(18), two years, no months, 18 days. The sample was phonetically transcribed using the guidelines given in Summary Box 2. During the first two listenings to the tape, the child's utterances were transcribed into a narrow phonetic transcription. On the third listening, interpretations were assigned when possible. Ambiguous words are placed in angle brackets and unclear parts in square brackets. Only clearly understood words are entered in the Lexicon.

One striking aspect of this sample in Table 3 is the amount of imitation that occurs. Here, imitation

Table 3. Part of a language sample from a young normal child, D, age 2;0(18)[a]

Transliterations (red ink)	Child's utterances (black and blue ink)	Adult utterances (black ink)
(father and child about to read a children's book) (green ink)		
		Here's the *Jolly Barnyard.* You know this book.
[ ]	41 [goʊbu]	
"pig"	42 [peɪt]	
		Yeah, pig.
"pig"	(43) [peɪg]	
"tape recorder"	44 [kʰeɪpʰukʰɔdə]	
		hm
"<what's it called>"	45 [hᵊzəzəkʰoʊ]	
"tape recorder"	46 [kʰikʰoʊdə]	
		What's happening here?
"tape recorder"	47 [kʰʌdə]	
		The man's carrying a basket of corn.
"corn"	(48) [kɔnə]	
		hmhm
"<[ ] corn>"	49 [haɪkʰoʊ]	
"the basket"	50 [dəbaɪsætʰ]	
"<oh [ ] eating>"	51 d [ɔɪjaeɪtinɛ]	
"cow"	52 [kʰaʊ]	
		They're eating.
"a boy"	53 [ʔʌbaɪ]	
		There's their sheep.
"sheep!"	(54) [si:pᵊ]	
		mhm
"[ ] sheep"	55 [gɪ:mʃip]	
"a sheep"	56 [ɪsip]	
<recorder>	57 [dədɛᵉᶦ]	
		That's a turkey.
"turkey"	(58) [tʰʌkʰi]	
		mmm
"oh duck!"	59 [oʊgatʰ]	
		Yeah, you're a duck.
"duck"	(60) [dʌkʰ]	
		You seem to put "s" on a lot of words, like ducks.
"ducks"	(61) [daks]	
		mm. You do both. Here's the chickens.
"chick"	(62) [tsɪk]	
"see doggy"	63 [dɪgagi]	
		Yeah, eating.
"eating <the> [ ]"	64 [ɪdinəwɪnə]	
"pillow"	65 [pʰoʊ]	
		Right there's the pillow.

[a]Entries should be recorded in different color inks (transliterations—red, child's utterances—black and blue, adult utterances—black, and situational descriptions—green) for clarity and quick identification. Because of constraints of printing, the colors are noted but not shown.

refers to any utterance produced after the adult has said the word, even if the child first produced it. The reason for this is that the child may change the pronunciation of the word because of the adult modeling. This, in fact, is exemplified in this sample by utterance 43 in which the child has now supplied a final [g]. (Utterances that have imitation have their numbers circled in the sample to record this fact.) Utterance 50, "the basket," is not circled because the child has not produced the word immediately after the adult. In this approach, imitation means immediate imitation.

To organize the Lexicon, the five steps in section 2.4.3 are followed. Step 1 is not necessary because the utterances are already numbered, in this case 41–65. The numbering begins with 41 because the sample has been taken from a larger sample. Because there are so few words, Step 2 can be done on a single page of paper or on index cards. If cards are used, we can first label one /p/ and enter "pig" from utterances 42 and 43, the latter entered inside a circle to keep track of the fact that it is imitated. The next card is marked /t/ and has "tape recorder" entered. This is done until all the clearly interpreted words have been entered. Below is a alphabetical listing of what each card would contain.

/A/   a   53, 56

/B/   2 boy   53
      1 basket   50

/C/   2 corn   (48)
      3 cow   52
      1 chick   (62)

/D/   2 duck   59, (60)
      3 ducks   (61)
      1 doggy   63

/E/   eating   (64)

/O/   oh   59

/P/   1 pig   42, (43)
      2 pillow   65

/S/   2 sheep   (54) 55, 56
      1 see   63

/T/   1 tape recorder
          44, 46, 47
      2 the   50
      3 turkey   (58)

Step 4 involves placing numbers within each card to the left of the words that give their alphabetical order. This has already been done in the above diagram. Obviously, no numbering is necessary for those cards with single entries, such as A, B, E, and O.

The last step, Step 5, is the important one that transfers the data to the Lexicon Sheet. The first card, A, contains just one word "a" with two occurrences. A check of the language sample shows these to be phonetically different, so they are each entered separately. This would give us:

lexical	phonetic	
A. a	ʌ -	
	ɪ -	

on the Lexicon Sheet (see sample 1, Lexicon Sheet 1, p. 19). The next entries, "basket" and "boy," have just one form each. The next card, /C/, has "chick" listed as the first entry. Because this is an imitation, however, it will need to be noted as such in red ink. Here, this is shown by an asterisk. Next, "corn" is entered, and then "cow." Because the latter has a diacritic feature of aspiration on it, this will be dropped when the word is placed on the Lexicon Sheet. Recall that only broad transcriptions are entered on this page. The rest of the items can be entered in this same way except for "sheep," which deserves some comment. Here we have three entries, which are [si:pᵊ], [ʃɪp], and [sɪp] from utterances 54, 55, and 56, respectively. First, we could consider all three imitations although our criteria, strictly applied, do not allow this because the adult utterance "mhm" intervenes. Next, when the first form is put into a broad transcription, it becomes [sɪp] and the same as the third form. We cannot enter this as one form occurring twice because one is considered imitated and the other is not, so they are entered separately.

Lexicon Sheet 1 (on p. 19) provides a complete lexicon for the sample given from child D with the second column showing only words that were produced spontaneously. Until we know more about the effects of imitation, it is suggested that analysis be done only with spontaneous words produced by the child. If imitated words constitute the majority of data obtained, then, of course, they must be included in the analysis. Last, this example shows how spontaneous language samples grudgingly yield data for phonological analysis, and shows why phonological diaries and articulation tests have dominated the literature on this topic.

2.6 PRACTICE DATA

Table 4 presents a selection of 25 utterances from a language sample taken when D was 2;8(26), or 8 months older than he was when the sample in Table 3 was taken. The sentences are both longer and clearer in Table 4, therefore, the data yields a larger set of data than that in Table 3. Attempt to use the four steps in section 2.4.3 to organize the lexicon for these data (use pencil). To aid in this, the following Practice Pages are provided: 1) a diagram that can be used in place of index cards for the initial entry (Step 2) of the words (Practice Page 2.1, p. 20), and 2) a blank lexicon sheet for Step 4 (Practice Page 2.2, p. 21). The final form of the data on the Lexicon Sheet is what would be used in subsequent phonological analyses. Appendix B contains the organization of these data and it can be referred to upon completion for checking to see if the steps have been correctly followed.

Table 4. Part of a language sample from a young normal child, D, age 2;8(26)

Transliteration	Child's utterances		Adult utterances
(a father and child about to read a children's book)			
"a airplane!"	144	[æˀ ɛəpweɪːn]	
			mhm
"that"	145	[æ]	
"this is the alligator"	146	[dɪs ɪz ᵈᶻbæːgeːər]	
			mhm
"this is a girl"	147	[dɪs ɪz ə̇ gɔːwə]	
			mhm
"this is a boat"	148	[dɪs ɪz ə boɶt]	
			Good
"this is a apple"	149	[dɪsɪz ə æːpʰɶɬ]	
			Good
"a apple"	150	[ʌ æːpʰ ɶ ɬ]	
			The boy, what's the boy doing?
"work"	151	[wɶ k]	
"he's grandma"	152	hiz [its gwæːma]	
			Pardon?
"he's grandma"	153	[hizgwæːma]	
			No he's not.
"there's grandma"	154	[dɛəz gwæːma]	
			mhm. It looks like a girl. Let's see what's on this page.
"there's a brat"	155	[dɛəz ə ræt°]	
"there's the bus"	156	[dɛəz dʌ bʌs]	
			mhm
(sound of a bus)	157	[m::]	
"there's the boat too"	158	[dɛəz dʌ boɶ t tʰu]	
			mhm what do you see? what's that?
"a clown"	159	[ʌ kwaɶ n]	
			yeah

continued

Table 4.—*continued*

Transliteration	Child's utterances	Adult utterances
"want have that birth-day cake cake"	160 [wənt hæv dæt bɔrt° deɪ kʰeɪktᵗ° keɪktᵗ°]	
"no I'll have that birthday cake on here"	161 [no ə + hæ dæt bɔrt°deɪ kʰeɪk ɔn hi:ə]	
		Yeah that would be nice, a little play. Let's see here, hm.
"these the doctor"	162 [diz dʌ daʔktər]	
		mhm
"in the bed"	163 [ɪn də bɛd]	
		Boy is sick.
"boy is sick"	⟨164⟩ [bɔɪ ɪz sɪk]	
"there the train"	165 [dɛə dɛəz dʌ [tʃeɪn]	mhm
"choo choo"	166 [tʃutʃu]	
		choo choo
"choo choo"	⟨167⟩ [tʃutʃu]	
(babbling)	168 [tʰu:du]	

LEXICON SHEET 1[a]

Child's name and age ___D 2;0 (18)___

types		types		types		types	
lexical	phonetic	lexical	phonetic	lexical	phonetic	lexical	phonetic
A. a	ʌ — ɪ —	A. a	ʌ — ɪ —				
B. basket	bəɪsæt	B basket	bəɪsæt				
boy	—baɪ	boy	—baɪ				
C. chick	*tsɪk	C. cow	kaʊ				
corn	*kɔnə	D. doggy	—gagi				
cow	kaʊ	duck	—gat				
D. doggy	—gagi	E. eating	ɪdin—				
duck	*dʌk	O. oh	oʊ				
	—gat	P. pig	peɪt				
ducks	*daks	pillow	poʊ				
E. eating	ɪdin —	S. see	dɪ —				
O. oh	oʊ	sheep	—ʃip				
P. pig	peɪt		—sip				
	*peɪg	T. tape-	keɪpu				
pillow	poʊ	recorder	kɔdə				
S. see	dɪ —		kikoʊdə				
sheep	*sip		kʌdə				
	—ʃip	the	də—				
	—sip						
T. tape-	keɪpu —						
recorder	kɔdə						
	kikoʊdə						
	kʌdə						
the	də—						
turkey	*tʌki						

[a]First column contains all utterances. Imitations are marked with an asterisk. The second column contains only spontaneous productions.

Organization of Data / 19

Practice Page 2.1   Record the lexical items from Table 4 onto these "file cards."

A

B

C

D

G

H

I

N

O

S

T

W

LEXICON SHEET

Transfer the data from the "cards"
(Practice Page 2.1) onto this Lexicon Sheet.

Child's name and age _D 2; 8 (26)_

types		types		types		types	
lexical	phonetic	lexical	phonetic	lexical	phonetic	lexical	phonetic

CHAPTER 3

Procedures for Phonetic Analysis

Glossary of Basic Terms

The following phonological data, as they would appear on a Lexicon Sheet, are provided for the purpose of exemplifying the definitions below.

"cat" [kæ] (2x)   "go"   [do]
       [dæ]   "that" [dæ]
"dog" [do] (3x)
       [dɔg]
       [dɔk]

lexical type: an adult word used by the child. There are four lexical types in these data—"cat," "dog," "go," "that."

phonetic token: any attempt to produce a lexical type. There are 10 phonetic tokens in these data.

phonetic type: a distinct phonetic shape for any particular lexical type. There are seven phonetic types: "cat" has two phonetic types, "dog" has three, and "go" and "that" have one each.

phonetic form: a distinct phonetic shape independent of lexical type. Here, there are five phonetic forms— [kæ] [dæ] [do] [dɔg] [dɔk]. The phonetic forms [dæ] and [do] each represent two phonetic types.

3.1 GOAL OF PHONETIC ANALYSIS

The goal of phonetic analysis is to establish the child's phonetic inventories for word initial, medial, and final position, and the frequency of preferred syllable shapes.

3.2 FORMS USED

Lexicon Sheet(s) (from which the data are taken)
Three Consonant Inventory Sheets—Phonetic Forms (one each for initial, medial, and final positions)
Child Syllable Sheet
Item and Replica Sheet
Summary Sheet

3.3 SUMMARY OF STEPS

Summary Box 3.   Steps in Phonetic Analysis

1. *Record the distribution of segments in the child's phonetic forms* (separately shown for word initial, medial, and final position on Consonant Inventory Sheets—Phonetic Forms).
2. *Determine the child's frequent syllable shapes* calculated on the Child Syllable Sheet and summarized on the Summary Sheet.
3. *Determine the frequency of the segments* (entered onto the Item and Replica Sheet, left side).
4. *Calculate the Criterion of Phonetic Frequency* (entered on the Summary Sheet).
5. *Summarize the most frequently used segments* (based on Criterion of Phonetic Frequency and entered onto Summary Sheet).
6. *Calculate measures of the child's phonetic ability* (entered on the Summary Sheet).

3.4 DISCUSSION OF PROCEDURES

A child's data that have been placed onto the Lexicon Sheet show the lexical types and phonetic types used by the child. They do not, however, show the separate phonetic forms. This is done by using the forms for phonetic analysis.

Step 1. **Record the distribution of segments in the child's phonetic forms (refer to Sample Analyses 3.3, 3.4, and 3.5 on pages 34–36)**

The first part of Step 1 of the Phonetic Analysis is to determine the child's phonetic forms by placing these according to their initial segment onto one of the Consonant Inventory Sheets. This provides us with a great deal of information on the child's preferred segments and syllable shapes, information that would be lacking if we examined only the child's phonological processes. The rest of Step 1 determines the frequency of medial and final segments. In the Phonetic Analysis, recall that initial, medial, and final segments refer to positions in the child's words, not syllables.

Step 1 has four parts:

1. Label a Consonant Inventory Sheet—Phonetic Forms to indicate initial position by checking the space for "initial." Also, enter the child's name and age.
2. Take each of the child's phonetic forms from the Lexicon Sheet and enter it onto the Consonant Inventory Sheet, with a separate box used for each distinct initial segment. The boxes are not labeled in advance because individual children may use several phonetic forms with the same initial segment, which would require the use of several boxes (c.f., Sample Analysis 3.3). A rough guide is to enter labial sounds in the first column boxes, dentals and alveolars in the second column, palatals in the third, and velars, glottals, and vowels in the fourth. Forms that begin with vowels go into a single box. Create new boxes if sounds not represented occur. Within the boxes, follow these guidelines:

a. CV syllables go into the left column.
b. CVC_1^n syllables go into the middle column (where C_1^n=one or more consonants).
c. Other syllables go into right column. Example:

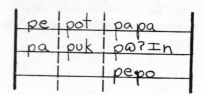

d. Information about how often a phonetic type occurs within a lexical type is not entered, e.g., "play" [peɪ] (3×) on the Lexicon Sheet is simply entered on the Consonant Inventory Sheet as [peɪ].
e. Consonant clusters are entered into separate boxes. For example, [pleɪ] is not placed in a box for [p] or [l] but in a separate box labeled [pl]. Example:

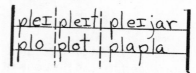

f. Keep track of phonetic types from a single lexical type that begin with the same sound, e.g., "dog" [dɔ] [dɔg] [dɔdɔ]. This is done to avoid later giving a sound "acquired status" if it is only in a few lexical types. This can be done by connecting the phonetic types with a tie-bar, or with braces, depending on whether the different phonetic types have the same syllable structure. Here are three different examples of this.

example of a tie-bar for
"dog" [dɔ] [dɔg] [dɔdɔ]

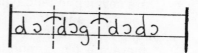

example of braces
for "dog" [dɔk] [dɔg]

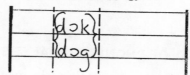

example of both tie-bar and braces, as in a lexical entry such as "cat" [kæ] [kæt] [kæk] [k æ k æ]

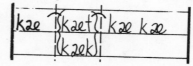

g. Record the number of times a phonetic form occurs across lexical types (i.e., when it is a homonym) by showing the number of lexical types it represents. For example, "plane" [pe], "play" [pe], and "plate" [pe] would be entered in the [p] box as

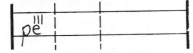

When this is done, circle these homonymous occurrences on the Lexicon Sheet in red ink, e.g., "plane" (pe), "play" (pe), and "plate" (pe). (Although the samples here and throughout the text are circled in black, circling in red ink is recommended for ease in recognizing the salient data.)

h. In some instances, a phonetic form will be homonymous, and also will be one of two or more variants for a lexical type, e.g., *phone* [pe], [pen], and *play* [pe], [pepe]. In these cases, a phonetic form may be entered more than once, but all entries after the first should be placed in parentheses to indicate redundancy. Example:

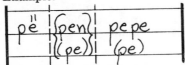

3. Repeat procedure for medial consonants—phonetic forms. This can be done by using a new Consonant Inventory Sheet—Phonetic Forms and taking the phonetic types from the Lexicon Sheet that contains medial consonants.

4. Repeat procedure for final consonants using a new Consonant Inventory Sheet and taking phonetic forms with final consonants directly from the Lexicon Sheet. Do not enter phonetic forms that end in a vowel.

After Step 1, there will be three Consonant Inventory Sheets that show the distribution of segments in the child's productions. The sheet for initial segments will contain all of the child's phonetic forms because all productions will have initial segments. Only some of the phonetic forms, however, will have medial and final consonants and thus will be entered onto the other two sheets. The next step is to record the frequency of the syllable types in the child's data.

Step 2. **Use the child's phonetic forms to determine the syllable shapes used by the child (refer to Sample Analysis 3.6 on page 37)**

Use the data recorded on the Consonant Inventory Sheet containing the initial segments of the child's phonetic forms. The syllable shapes of the child's Phonetic Forms are calculated separately for each initial segment and are entered on the Child Syllable Sheet. The Child Syllable Sheet is divided into monosyllables and multisyllables (which here means two or more syllables). The monosyllables are CV, e.g., [kæ], CVC, e.g., [kæt], CVC_2^n where C_2^n indicates two or more

consonants, e.g., [kæts] [peɪnts], $C_2^n VC_0^n$ where C_2^n indicates an initial cluster and C_0^n represents whatever consonants that may follow, or none, e.g., [pleɪ], [plot], [plast], V, e.g., [a], VC, e.g., [ap], and VC_2^n, e.g., [ats]. The disyllables include complete CVCV reduplication, e.g., [kaka], partial CVCV reduplication, e.g., [papi], or [putu] where either the vowels or the consonants are the same. Partial reduplication occurs for VCV when the vowels are the same, e.g., [apa], versus nonreduplicated VCV [api]. Also, there is nonreduplicated CVCV, e.g., [dati], [pabu]. The definitions of reduplication here are taken from Schwartz, Leonard, Wilcox, and Folger (1980). Other multisyllabic shapes are Other Reduplications (other than CVCV ones), such as [tɪk tɪk], [badu badu], CVCVC [badɛt] and other multisyllables, e.g., [kipba], [kadibu]. Follow these guidelines:

1. Put in the number of times each syllable shape is used for each initial segment, beginning with [m].
2. Enter the syllable shape of phonetic forms beginning with consonant clusters separately. Blanks are provided at the bottom of the left-hand column for this.
3. Calculate the totals for each syllable shape at the bottom of the page. Calculate the total number of phonetic forms per initial segment in the right-hand column. The calculation of the total number of syllable shapes and the total number of phonetic forms should be the same.

Step 3. **Determine the frequency of the segments (also refer to Sample Analysis 3.2, on page 33)**

1. Using the Consonant Inventory Sheet, count the frequency of each initial speech sound and enter it in the top far left display, on the Item and Replica Sheet, labeled *word initial segments*. Example: the following is part of one such display of a hypothetical child, and indicates that there was one phonetic type beginning with [m], two with [p], twenty with [b], twenty-one with [t], and none with [d].

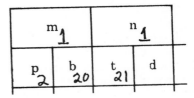

a. In cases with phonetic types enclosed in braces, or connected by a tie-bar, two counts are made. These are: number of phonetic forms/number of lexical types.

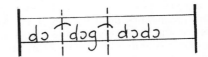

Here, we would enter d 3/1 on the Item and Replica Sheet to show there were three phonetic types but only one lexical type. This is done so that we will not count a segment as "frequent" in case it is only used in one word.

b. In cases with multiple phonetic types, two counts are also made. These are the same as above, that is, number of phonetic forms/number of phonetic types (or lexical types). Example:

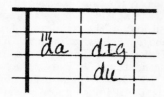

Here, we would enter d 3/5 because there are three phonetic forms for five phonetic or lexical types (or words). This is done so that we do not count a sound as "frequent" if it occurs in many words but is always in the same phonetic context. When counting the number of lexical types, do not count again those phonetic forms that are in parentheses. Example:

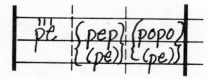

In this display, there are three phonetic forms, [pe], [pep], and [popo], and three lexical types; we do not count the cases of [pe] in parentheses because they are already counted in [p̈e].

c. If a segment occurs for which there is no labeled box on the Item and Replica Sheet, enter it in an appropriate space and enter its frequency. For example, if [ŋ] occurs twice initially, it can be shown as follows:

m		n				ŋ₂	
p	b	t	d	tʃ	dӡ	k	g

d. Count consonant clusters separately and make new boxes for them.

2. Repeat these steps with medial consonants and enter frequencies into left central display on Item and Replica Sheet.

3. Repeat these steps with final consonants and enter frequencies into left bottom display on the Item and Replica Sheet.

When Step 3 is completed, we will have compiled the phonetic data and counted the frequency of the different consonants used by the child. At this point, however, the data only show a range of frequencies from those sounds that never occur, to those that occur only once and to those that are quite frequent. If it is left like this, there is always the possibility that infrequent sounds may have been fortuitous produc-

tions on the child's part, or even errors in transcription, and not part of the child's articulatory repertoire. The next step, then, is designed to determine a criterion, arbitrary as it may be, that will allow us to eliminate infrequent from frequent productions.

Step 4. Calculate the Criterion of Phonetic Frequency

1. From the Lexicon Sheet, count the number of lexical types, phonetic types, and phonetic tokens in the data, and enter these numbers on the top of the Summary Sheet. Take the number of phonetic forms from the Child Syllable Sheet and enter this onto the Summary Sheet also. When counting phonetic types, disregard those that only differ by syllable position. For example, plane [-pe] [-pe-] will be numbered as one phonetic type.

2. On the Summary Sheet, determine the Criterion of Frequency. First, add together the number of lexical types and phonetic forms and divide the total by 2. Next, divide this number by 25 and round off to the nearest whole number. (This figure is based on the arbitrary assumption that any sound used by the child should at least occur once in any random selection of 25 phonetic forms or lexical types.)

For example, a sample of 120 lexical types and 100 phonetic forms will have the following calculation on the Summary Sheet:

Criterion of Frequency _____4_____ $(\frac{220}{2} = \frac{110}{25})$

This criterion is considered both a measure of the ability to produce a sound and the tendency to use it. With it, we can then establish the child's functional phonetic inventory.

3. If the Criterion of Frequency is 1, use 2 as a minimum criterion.

Step 5. Determine the child's frequent segments

1. Circle in red all the sounds on the Item and Replica Sheet (in the top left display) that meet the criterion of frequency. If two numbers are given, use the lower number, for example, for 3/5, use 3. These are considered acquired sounds.

2. Put in parentheses on the Item and Replica Sheet, again in red ink, those sounds—called transition sounds—that would meet the criterion if their frequency when divided by the criterion would round off to 1. For example, if [b] occurs four times and the criterion is 5, 4/5=0.80, which rounds to 1. To expedite this calculation, Table 5 can be used.

3. Put an asterisk, in red, on the Item and Replica Sheet for each time a sound meets the Criterion of Frequency more than once. For example, if [b] occurs 24 times and the criterion is 5, 24/5=4 less 1 equals three times beyond criterion (do not round off) and [b] would be shown as b***.

4. Enter the information just determined on the Item and Replica Sheet onto the Summary Sheet in the space under the heading *word initial*. For example, the following is a hypothetical display from an Item and Replica Sheet when circles, parentheses,

Table 5. Frequencies of acquired and transition sounds

Criterion of frequency	Transitional frequencies	Doubled frequencies
2	none	4 or more
3	2	6 or more
4	2, 3	8 or more
5	3, 4	10 or more
6	3, 4, 5	12 or more
7	4, 5, 6	14 or more
8	4, 5, 6, 7	16 or more
9	5, 6, 7, 8	18 or more
10	5, 6, 7, 8, 9	20 or more

and asterisks have been entered based on a Criterion of Frequency of 5.

Word initial segments

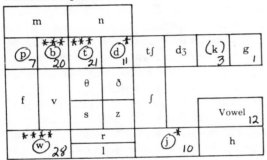

They would be entered on the Summary Sheet as follows, keeping the same spatial positions:

word initial _____

p $b^{\star\uparrow\star}$ $t^{\star\star\star}$ $d^{\star}$ (k)

$w^{\star\star\star\star}$ $j^{\uparrow}$

5. Repeat all steps with word medial consonants, using the middle left display on the Item and Replica Sheet and entering the summary on the Summary Sheet next to *word medial*.
6. Repeat all steps with word final consonants, using the bottom left display on the Item and Replica Sheet and entering the summary on the Summary Sheet next to *word final*.
   At the end of this step we have a phonetic inventory for the child that can be compared to that of other children and to the same child when later samples are taken to see if improvement has taken place. The next step is the last step dealing with phonetic segments; it calculates quantitative measures that can be used as a gross measure of phonetic progress.

Step 6. **Calculate the measures of the child's phonetic ability**

1. Calculate the child's Total Number of Sounds.
   a. Using the phonetic inventory shown on the Summary Sheet, count the number of sounds that meet criterion for word initial position.

Enter this in the blank after *word initial*. For example, in the example above in Step 5,4, the number 6 will be entered because six sounds reached criterion, (p, b, t, d, w, j).

b. Count the number of sounds in parentheses and place it in parentheses next to above count. In the above example, only [k] is in parentheses, so we would enter 6(1).

c. Repeat step for phonetic inventory shown for *word medial*. Repeat step for phonetic inventory shown as *word final*.

d. Total the counts from the three word positions and enter these in the blank on the Summary Sheet labeled *Total Number of Sounds*. Example.

Total Number of Sounds   9(4)

word initial 4(2)   word medial 2(1)   word final 3(1)

$m^{\star}$ n m $n^{\star}$ p

$p^{\star}b$ (t) (K) (t) f $s^{\star}$ (f)

Do not count vowels in count for initial sounds, so that the count is only of the consonant inventory.

This measure of Total Number of Sounds is used as a gross measure of phonetic development. Presumably, the more sounds a child can use, the more advanced he or she is in articulation. Recall that this is based on a broad phonetic transcription. Children who show widespread phonetic instability will usually do so at a more narrow phonetic level.

2. Calculate the child's Articulation Score. This is a more precise score than the Total Number of Sounds. It is obtained as follows:

Articulation score = 3 × all acquired sounds with asterisks

2 × all acquired sounds without asterisks

1 × all transition sounds, i.e., those in parentheses
——————
Total

Here, points are assigned for sounds used by the child, with frequent ones getting the heaviest weight. For example, the Articulation Score (AS) for the hypothetical sample above, Step 6,1.d would be:

Total 26 (AS)

word initial	word medial	word final
3 × 2 (m*, p*) = 6	3 × 1 (n*) = 3	3 × 1 (s*) = 3
2 × 2 (n, b) = 4	2 × 1 (m) = 2	2 × 2 (p, f) = 4
1 × 2 ((t, k)) = 2	1 × 1 ((t)) = 1	1 × 1 ((f)) = 1
Total 12	6	8

3. Determine the measures of frequency for syllable types. Under Most Frequent Syllable Types enter the two most frequent types and then actual frequency, e.g., CV (27), CVC (12). Next, calculate the Proportion of Monosyllables. This is the number of monosyllables divided by the total number of syllable types (or phonetic forms). For example, if there are 60 phonetic forms and 30 are monosyllables, the proportion is up 30/60 or 0.50. This proportion gives us an idea about the child's ability to

produce multisyllabic forms. Last, calculate the Proportion of Closed Syllables. Here, this is a limited measure of the number of CV and CVC syllables divided into the number of CVC syllables. For example, if there are 20 CV forms, and 20 CVC forms, the proportion will be 20/40 or 0.50. This measure will give us at least an approximate idea of the child's ability to use final consonants.

3.5   SAMPLE PHONETIC ANALYSIS

Lexicon Sheet 2 (page 31) provides data from a phonological diary of the speech of my daughter Jennika who was age 1;5 at the time. These data will be used to demonstrate the phonetic analysis described in this chapter. To follow the discussion, the reader should recall the steps described in section 3.4 and refer to pages 24–27.

The first part of Step 1 is to label a Consonant Inventory Sheet—Phonetic Forms—Initial segments, and also enter the child's name and age, as has been done in Sample Analysis 3.3. Next, enter the child's phonetic forms from the Lexicon Sheet onto the Consonant Inventory Sheet. Starting with the first phonetic form on the Lexicon Sheet, we see that the first four all begin with vowels, so they all go into the vowel box on the Consonant Inventory Sheet, which is arbitrarily placed in the lower right corner. Also, because all of them are disyllables, they will go into the third column. Also, braces are needed to enclose the forms for *alldone* and *apple*. The next series of words begins with [b] and will go into the [b] box, started in the left column. The first Phonetic Form [bat] goes into the second column because it is CVC. The next three, [bɪ], [baɪ], and [bi] all go into the first column because they are CV. Next, we have 6 phonetic types for the word *blanket*. Recall that Step 1,2.(f) indicates that different phonetic types from the same lexical type are either placed together and enclosed in braces or connected by tie-bars to indicate this fact. First, because four of the phonetic types begin with [bw], a separate box is started for these, as stated in Step 1,2.e (c.f., Sample analysis 3.3). A combination of tie-bars and parentheses is used to enter these as follows:

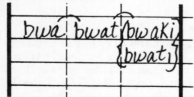

These show that there are four phonetic types for one lexical type. Next, [bat] and [bati] are entered into the *b* box. Notice that [bat] already occurs in this column because it was also used for "bat." We therefore have one phonetic form representing two lexical types. To show this, we enter [bat[11]] where '11' means that it occurs for two lexical types. To show that [bat] occurred within the same lexical type as [bati], a tie-bar connects the two of them. Last, we need to show the homonymy of [bat] by circling (in red) both of its occurrences on the Lexicon Sheet, as indicated by Step 1,2.g. This has already been done on Lexicon Sheet 2. The entry for "blanket" is usually complicated but shows all the possible variant possibilities of Step 1,2.

The next word, "book," also has several phonetic types that require the use of tie-bars and braces. It is important to understand how its phonetic types have been entered because it shows all the possibilities. The rest of the data can be entered in the same fashion. To finish the "b" words, the child's [batʃ] for "box" will go into the second column of the *b* box, and the two phonetic types for "bye-bye" will go in the third column and will be enclosed in braces. Jennika's 1;5 Sample Analysis 3.3 shows all the phonetic types entered.

The next Steps, 1,3. and 1,4., involve taking the relevant phonetic forms from the Lexicon Sheet and entering these onto two separate Consonant Inventory Sheets for medial and final consonants. There are only a few medial consonants in these data, and their entries are shown in Jennika 1;5, Sample Analysis 3.4. The phonetic forms for final consonants for Jennika's data are on Sample Analysis 3.5. When all the phonetic forms are entered onto these three Consonant Inventory Sheets, Step 1 is completed.

In Step 2, we examine the distribution of syllable structure in Jennika. On the Child Syllable Sheet, enter the number of syllable types that occur on the data taken from the Consonant Inventory Sheet that shows initial segments. Beginning with [m], there are three that are CV, one that is CVC, and one that is CVCV, for a total of five. The figures are entered box by box, and only phonetic forms that are not in parentheses are counted. For vowels, enter these under the vowel columns, separated from the other syllable shapes at the bottom of the page. Because a cluster [bw] has occurred, this is added at the bottom of the sheet before a blank row and its frequency also is placed in the *cluster* column. The totals for the rows and columns are then calculated and entered in the appropriate blanks on the Summary Sheet (see Sample Analysis 3.6).

In Step 3, we count the occurrence of the numbers of phonetic forms and lexical types that are reported on the Consonant Inventory Sheets and enter these numbers on the left side of the Item and

Replica Sheet. Beginning with initial segments, enter 5/3 for "m" because there are five phonetic forms, but these represent only three lexical types because [mɔ] [mo] and [mʌ] all are for the same word or lexical type and are enclosed in parentheses. Also, "b" has the largest number of phonetic forms—15—and these are used for nine lexical types. The sound [dʒ] has four phonetic forms, but these are for just one word—"juice"—so they are listed 4/1. It is for cases like this one that both phonetic forms and lexical types are counted so that a sound occurs in different words before it is claimed to be acquired. After counting initial segments, the medial and then final consonant forms are counted and entered on the Item and Replica Sheet (c.f., Sample Analysis 3.2).

We are now ready to proceed to Step 4 to determine the Criterion of Frequency. First, enter information about sample size at the top of the Summary Sheet. The lexical types and phonetic types, which come to 42 and 73, respectively, are numbered on the Lexicon Sheet. The number of phonetic tokens is the number of phonetic types plus their repeated occurrences as indicated in parentheses after the phonetic types on the Lexicon Sheet. For example, [ædʌm] occurred two times, and [bwati] twice. These repeated occurrences bring the number of lexical tokens to 90. The number of phonetic forms, taken from the Child Syllable Sheet, is 70. (The number of phonetic forms can also be determined by adding the numbers entered under *initial segments* on the Item and Replica Sheet. When two numbers are given, for example, 5/3, the far left one is counted.) To determine the Criterion of Frequency, use the formula described in Step 4,2. and repeated on the Summary Sheet. First, add the number of lexical types and phonetic forms, 42 and 70, respectively, for a total of 112, then divide this by 2, for 56. This figure, divided by 25, gives 2.2 or 2 as the Criterion of Frequency (see Sample Analysis 3.1).

The Criterion of Frequency is used to determine the child's phonetic inventory. First, circle (in red) all the sounds on the Item and Replica Sheet that occur two or more times, using the lower number if two are given. For example, [dʒ] is shown as 4/1 and is not circled because the lower number, one, is below the criterion. Next, we would parenthesize transitional sounds, but here there are none, because the guidelines do not allow transitional sounds with frequencies less than 2 (c.f., Table 5). The last notation to make on the Item and Replica Sheet is the placing of an asterisk for each time a sound meets the Criterion of Frequency after the first time. For example, initial [b] occurs in 9 lexical types, so 9/2= 4−1=3. Thus, [b] takes three asterisks. The circles and asterisks for

Jennika are shown on Sample Analysis 3.1. This information is then summarized on the Summary Sheet. For Jennika, it is as follows:

Total Number of Sounds _____ Criterion of Frequency _____ ($\overline{2} = \overline{25}$)
word initial _____ word medial _____ word final _____

m
p   b***   d***   p b t*   d***   m*   t**   tʃ
w*

The first part of the last step, the calculation of the Total Number of Sounds, consists simply of adding the number of sounds that reach criterion and, separately, adding the numbers in parentheses (which is not necessary in this case) and then showing these totals first for word position, then in total. For the above data, the totals are: 5 for initial position (vowel is not counted), 4 for medial position, and 3 for final position. The total, which can be used as a gross measure of development, is 12. Enter all these totals on the Summary Sheet.

The Articulation Score can be calculated next, and would be as follows:

word initial _____   word medial _____   word final _____
$3 \times 3 (b,d,w)$ = 9 $3 \times 2 (t,d)$ = 6 $3 \times 2 (m,t,)$ = 6
$2 \times 2 (m,p)$ = 4 $2 \times 2 (p,b)$ = 4 $2 \times 1 (tʃ)$ = 2
_____   _____   _____
13   10   8

The Articulation Score is then entered on the Summary Sheet.

Last, enter the quantified information on syllable structure. The two most frequent syllable shapes are CV (17) and CVC and CVCV (13 each). The proportion of monosyllables is the number of monosyllables, 40, divided by 70, the total number of phonetic forms for 0.57. The proportion of closed syllables is calculated by dividing the number of CVC forms, 13, by the total of CV and CVC's (or 17+13= 30), for 0.43. Enter all of these on the Summary Sheet (c.f., Sample Analysis 3.1). Chapter 7 describes some norms for the interpretation of these figures.

3.6   PRACTICE DATA

Lexicon Sheet 3 contains data from a language-delayed child, R, at age 3;11. The transcription has been broadened based on the procedures described in Chapter 2. This broadening has led to the elimination of vowel lengthening, yet other features remain the same.

These data are provided for the reader to use in attempting to do a phonetic analysis firsthand. For this purpose, the next pages contain blank analysis sheets to be used according to the instructions in section 3.3. Follow the steps given in section 3.3 and attempt to do a phonetic analysis of these data onto the blank sheets. Appendix C contains an analysis of the data that can be referred to after each step, and also contains a brief commentary on the nature of the data and the unique problems they pose for doing analyses. Afterward, compare the results of this language-delayed child's productions to that of Jennika at age 1;5. Decide whether they are the same or not, then see the final remarks in Appendix C.

Used for sample phonetic
analysis on the following pages.

Child's name and age __Jennika   1;5__

	types			types			types			types		
lexical	phonetic		lexical	phonetic		lexical	phonetic		lexical	phonetic	

lexical	phonetic	lexical	phonetic	lexical	phonetic	lexical	phonetic
1. all done	¹ædʌm(2x)	15. down	³¹ daʊ	35. rock	⁶¹ (wa)		
	² ɔdʌm		³² dʌm		⁶² watɪ		
2. apple	³ apʊ	16. egg	³³ i	36. see	⁶³ si (2x)		
	⁴ æpɑl	17. eye	³⁴ (aI)	37. shoe	⁶⁴ ʃu (2x)		
3. bath	⁵ (bat)	18. get down	³⁵ didʌm	38. spoon	⁶⁵ pʌm		
4. bib	⁶ bɪ	19. hat	³⁶ atʃ (2x)	39. sweater	⁶⁶ waʃ		
5. bike	⁷ baI		³⁷ aItʃ		⁶⁷ watʃ		
6. bird	⁸ bi	20. hot	³⁸ at	40. up	⁶⁸ ap (3x)		
7. blanket	⁹ bwa		³⁹ ati		⁶⁹ ʌp		
	¹⁰ (bat)	21. hi	⁴⁰ aIdi		⁷⁰ api (2x)		
	¹¹ bwaki		⁴¹ (aI)(2x)	41. walk	⁷¹ at		
	¹² bwati (2x)		⁴² haI	42. water	⁷² wawa		
	¹³ bwat	22. icecream	⁴³ dʒu dʒu		⁷³ wʌwʌ		
	¹⁴ bati	23. juice	⁴⁴ dʒu (2x)				
8. book	¹⁵ ba (2x)		⁴⁵ dʒus (2x)				
	¹⁶ bʌ (2x)		⁴⁶ dʒut				
	¹⁷ ba?	24. kitty	⁴⁷ dɪti				
	¹⁸ bat (2x)	25. Kristen	⁴⁸ dɪdɪn				
	¹⁹ bʌt	26. mommy	⁴⁹ mami				
9. box	²⁰ batʃ	27. move	⁵⁰ mɔ				
10. bye bye	²¹ babaI		⁵¹ mo				
	²² bəbaI		⁵² mʌ				
11. chair	²³ dʃ	28. mouth	⁵³ maʊt				
12. cookie	²⁴ duti (2x)	29. no	⁵⁴ no				
	²⁵ didi (2x)	30. out	⁵⁵ aʊ				
	²⁶ dodi	31. pee	⁵⁶ pipi				
	²⁷ digi	32. poop	⁵⁷ bʌbo				
	²⁸ gigi		⁵⁸ bʌbu				
13. daddy	²⁹ dædi	33. ride	⁵⁹ waI				
14. dog	³⁰ dɔdi	34. ring rosy	⁶⁰ (wa)				

Sample Analysis 3.1   SUMMARY SHEET

Child's name and age __Jennika 1;5__

| Sample size | lexical types: _42_ | phonetic types: _73_ | phonetic tokens: _90_ | phonetic forms: _70_ |

Phonetic Analysis   Articulation Score _31_

Total Number of Sounds _12_   Criterion of Frequency _2_   ($\frac{112}{2} = \frac{56}{25}$)

word initial _5_   word medial _4_   word final _3_

m
p b ✱✱✱   d ✱✱✱   p b ✝✱ d ✱✱✱   m ✱
w ✱   ✝ ✱✱
                                                                        ✝s

| syllable types: | most frequent: | CV (17) | Proportion of: | _0.57_ | Monosyllables _0.43_ | Closed syllables |
| | | CVC (13) | | | | |

Analysis of Homonymy

Ratio of Homonymous forms _____:1   Homonymous types _____:1

Proportion of Homonymous forms _____   Homonymous types _____

Substitution Analysis

	m	n	ŋ	p	b	t	d	k	g	tʃ	dʒ	f	θ	s	ʃ	v	ð	z	ʒ	w	j	r	l	h		
I			▓																▓							
A																										
F																				▓	▓			▓		

Proportion of Data _____ (/67) and Matches _____ (/) Acquired sounds _____

Phonological Process Analysis   Number of:_____ Processes_____ Affected Segments

FINAL CONSONANT DELETION

REDUCTION OF CONSONANT CLUSTERS

SYLLABLE DELETION AND REDUPLICATION

FRONTING OF PALATALS AND VELARS

STOPPING OF FRICATIVES AND AFFRICATES

SIMPLIFICATION OF LIQUIDS AND NASALS

OTHER PROCESSES

| 0.0–0.20 | 0.21–0.49 | 0.50–0.79 | 0.80–.100 |

Sample Analysis 3.2

Child's name and age _Jennika 1;5_

Child's Phonetic Inventory

Word initial segments

(m) 5/3		n 1		b w 4/1			
(p)	(b) *** 5/?	t	(d) *** 12/8	t∫	dʒ 4/1	k	g 1
f	v	θ s	ð z 1	∫ 1		Vowel 15/10	
(w) * 7/5		r l		j		h 1	

Word medial consonants

m 1		n			ŋ		
(p) 4/3	(b) 4/2	(t) * 6/5	(d) ** 9/7	t∫	dʒ 1	k 1	g 2/1
f	v	θ s	ð z	∫	3		
w 2/1		r l		j		h	

Word final consonants

(m) 5/4		n 1			ŋ		
p 2/1	b	(t) 7/7	d	(t∫) 4/3	dʒ	k	g
f	v	θ s 1	ð z	∫	3		?
		r l 1	ɾ ɭ 1				

Child's Substitutions

Syllable initial consonants

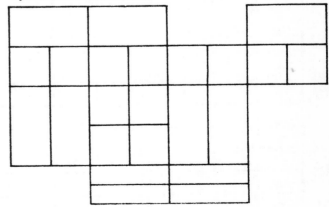

Ambisyllabic consonants

Syllable final consonants

CONSONANT INVENTORY SHEET
Phonetic Forms   Child's name and age _Jennika 1;5_

{mɔ} {mo} {mʌ}	mæt	mami	no					
bɪ baɪ bi {ba} {bʌ}	bät (bat) bati batʃ {bɑhaɪ} {baˀ}{bəhaɪ} {bɒˀ}{bʌho} (bʌt)(bʌbu)	dɛ daʊˀdʌm	(duti) {didi} {dodi} (digi) dæɪdi dɔdi didʌm dɪti dɪdɪn	dʒuˀ{dʒʊʃ} {dʒuˀ}	dʒudʒʊ			gigi
	pʌm	pipi						
bwa ˀbwat{bwaki} (bwati)						haɪ		
waɪ {waʃ}{wati} wä {watʃ}((wa) {wawa} (wʌwʌ)						i {atʃ}{ædʌm} aɪ {aɪtʃ}{ɔdʌm} aʊ {apu} {ap}{æpɒl} {ʌpˀ} api		
				ʃu		{at}ˀ ati atˀ {aɪdi} (aɪ)		

CONSONANT INVENTORY SHEET
Phonetic Forms   Child's name and age _Jennika 1;5_

_____ initial   ✓ medial   _____ final

mami							
{ apʊ } { æpɒl } pipi api		{ bwati } { bati } duti ati dɪti wati				bwaki
{ babaɪ } { bəbaɪ } { bʌbo } { bʌbʌ }		{ æedʌm } { ɔdʌm } { didi } { dodi } dædi dɔdi didʌm ɑɪdi dɪdɪn		dʒudʒu		{ digi } { gigi }
{ wʌwʌ } { wawa }						

CONSONANT INVENTORY SHEET
Phonetic Forms Child's name and age Jennika 1;5

____ initial   ____ medial   ✓ final

pʌm {ædʌm}			dɪdɪn			
dʌm {ɔdʌm}						
didʌm						
{ap}		at" bäät		batʃ		ba?
{ʌp}		(bat) bwat		{atʃ}		
		{bɒt} mæt		(aɪtʃ)		
		(bʌt)		watʃ		
		dʒut				
				waʃ		
		æpɒl				

CHILD SYLLABLE SHEET

Child's name and age Jennika 1;5

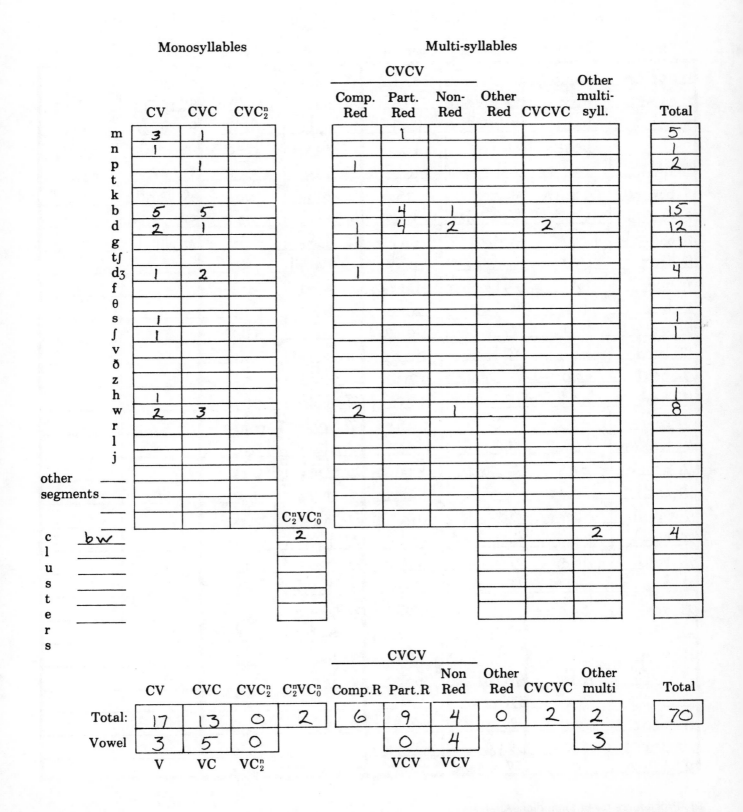

Monosyllables

Multi-syllables

	CV	CVC	CVC$_2^n$	CVCV Comp. Red	Part. Red	Non-Red	Other Red	CVCVC	Other multi-syll.	Total
m	3	1			1					5
n	1									1
p		1		1						2
t										
k										
b	5	5			4	1				15
d	2	1		1	4	2		2		12
g				1						1
tʃ										
dʒ	1	2		1						4
f										
θ										
s	1									1
ʃ	1									1
v										
ð										
z										
h	1									1
w	2	3		2		1				8
r										
l										
j										
other segments ____										
____										
____										

clusters

		C$_2^n$VC$_0^n$						CVCVC	Total
bw		2						2	4

Totals

	CV	CVC	CVC$_2^n$	C$_2^n$VC$_0^n$	CVCV Comp.R	Part.R	Non Red	Other Red	CVCVC	Other multi	Total
Total:	17	13	0	2	6	9	4	0	2	2	70
Vowel	3	5	0			0	4			3	
	V	VC	VC$_2^n$			VCV	VCV				

Use for Practice Page 3.1–3.6.   LEXICON SHEET 3

Child's name and age R 3;11

types		types		types		types	
lexical	phonetic	lexical	phonetic	lexical	phonetic	lexical	phonetic
1. apple	hæpo	29. duck	gʌk	55. moon	mu	83. waffle	pafo
2. arm	nan	30. elephant	tʌtʌt	56. one	wʌn	84. water	dʌdo
3. baby	behi	31. feet	pat	57. paper	peto	85. web	wɛp
	bebe	32. fire	ha	58. pear	peo	86. whale	weo
4. ball	po	33. fireman	hanan	59. pie	paɪ	87. wheel	heo
5. banana	nænʌ	34. fish	pʌsə	60. robe	wop	88. whistle	pɛsɪf
6. basket	sʌkə(2x)	35. flower	ha	61. rock	wak	89. window	dʌdo
7. bathtub	bʌfʌt	36. foot	pat	62. safe	fef	90. witch	wɪtʃ
8. bear	peo	37. fork	pak	63. seagull	sigo		
9. bed	tʌt	38. hammer	næno	64. seed	sit		
10. bee	bi	39. hand	nan	65. shoe	suwə		
11. belt	tap	40. hat	hat(2x)		sup		
12. bird	bo	41. high	haɪ	66. shovel	tʌbo		
13. boat	tap	42. horsie	hɔrsi	67. slide	taɪ		
14. book	bʌk		sɔrsi	68. snake	sek		
15. boy	pɔɪ		sʌsi	69. spider	dʌdo		
16. broom	num	43. house	haʊs	70. star	da		
17. brush	bʌʃ	44. king	kin	71. stick	sʌk		
18. butter	dʌdo		kɪn	72. stove	dov		
19. candy	dægi	45. kitty cat	kitat	73. table	tebo		
20. comb	kom	46. ladder	dado	74. tail	tejo		
21. cow	daʊ	47. letter	tato	75. tea	ti		
22. cup	pat	48. light	taɪt	76. teeth	tʌf		
23. desk	sʌk		daɪt	77. telephone	tʌpo		
24. doctor	gaga	49. man	næn	78. tent	tat		
25. dog	kak(2x)		nan	79. too	to		
	dɔk	50. marble	babo	80. top	tat		
	gak	51. meat	mit		pat		
26. door	do	52. milk	naʊk	81. towel	taʊ		
27. dress	sæs	53. mommy	mami(2x)		tajo		
28. drum	lam	54. mommy	mama	82. tractor	gago		

SUMMARY SHEET

Child's name and age ___R   3;11___

| Sample size | lexical types: ___ | phonetic types: ___ | phonetic tokens: ___ | phonetic forms: ___ |

Phonetic Analysis   Articulation Score ___

Total Number of Sounds _____   Criterion of Frequency _____   ($\overline{2} = \overline{25}$)
word initial _____   word medial _____   word final _____

syllable types: ___   most frequent: ___   Proportion of: ___   Monosyllables ___   Closed syllables

Analysis of Homonymy
Ratio of Homonymous forms ___:1   Homonymous types ___:1
Proportion of Homonymous forms _____   Homonymous types _____

Substitution Analysis

	m	n	ŋ	p	b	t	d	k	g	tʃ	dʒ	f	θ	s	ʃ	v	ð	z	ʒ	w	j	r	l	h		
I			▒																▒						___	
A																									___	
F																				▒	▒		▒		___	

Proportion of Data _____ (/67) and Matches _____ (/) Acquired sounds _____

Phonological Process Analysis   Number of:_____ Processes _____ Affected Segments

FINAL CONSONANT DELETION

REDUCTION OF CONSONANT CLUSTERS

SYLLABLE DELETION AND REDUPLICATION

FRONTING OF PALATALS AND VELARS

STOPPING OF FRICATIVES AND AFFRICATES

SIMPLIFICATION OF LIQUIDS AND NASALS

OTHER PROCESSES

| 0.0–0.20 | 0.21–0.49 | 0.50–0.79 | 0.80–.100 |

ITEM AND REPLICA SHEET

Child's name and age _____ R   3;11 _____

Child's Phonetic Inventory

Word initial segments

m		n					
p	b	t	d	tʃ	dʒ	k	g
f	v	θ / s	ð / z	ʃ		Vowel	
w		r / l		j		h	

Word medial consonants

m		n				ŋ	
p	b	t	d	tʃ	dʒ	k	g
f	v	θ / s	ð / z	ʃ	ʒ		
w		r / l		j		h	

Word final consonants

m		n				ŋ	
p	b	t	d	tʃ	dʒ	k	g
f	v	θ / s	ð / z	ʃ	ʒ		
		r / l		ɾ / ɭ			

Child's Substitutions

Syllable initial consonants

Ambisyllabic consonants

Syllable final consonants

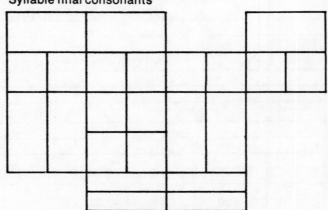

Practice Page 3.3

CONSONANT INVENTORY SHEET
Phonetic Forms   Child's name and age _R 3; 11_____

__✓__ initial   _____ medial   _____ final

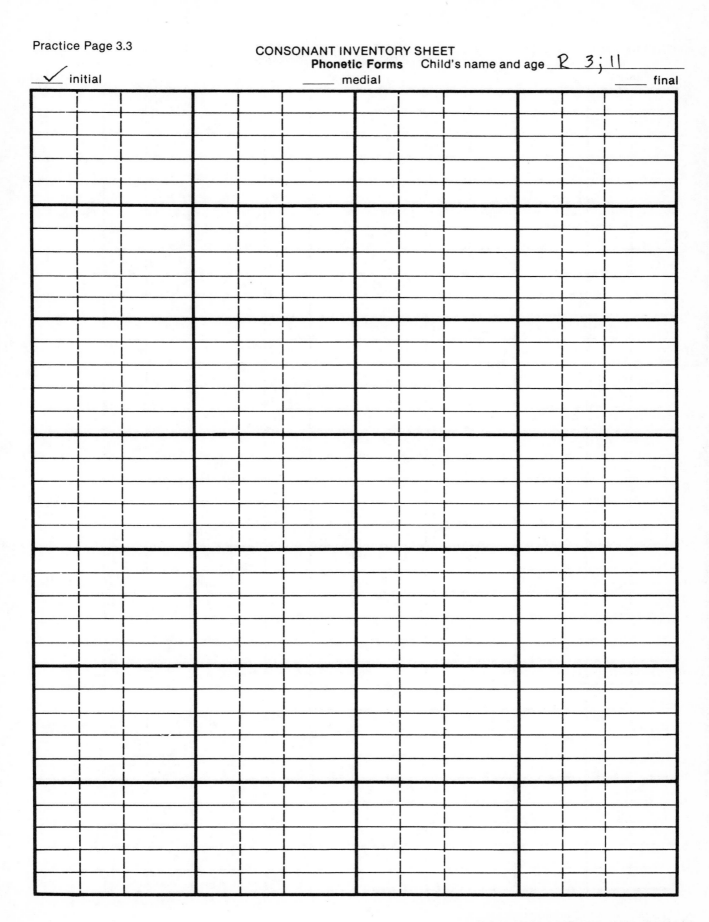

CONSONANT INVENTORY SHEET

Phonetic Forms   Child's name and age _R 3;11_

_____ initial   _____ medial   ✓ final

CONSONANT INVENTORY SHEET
Phonetic Forms   Child's name and age _R   3; 11_

_____ initial   ✓ medial   _____ final

CHAPTER 4

The Analysis of Homonymy

Glossary of Basic Terms

homonymy: when two different words have the same phonetic form, for example, *fair* and *fare* in adult English, or *ring* and *wring*

child homonymy: when the child produces the same phonetic form for two or more adult words that normally are not homonymous, for example, Jennika (at age 1;5) [bat] for *bath* and *blanket*

homonymous form: a phonetic form of the child's that represents two or more lexical types, for example, [bat] in Jennika (at age 1;5) is a homonymous form

homonymous type: a lexical type that has a homonymous form as one of its phonetic types, for example, in Jennika (at age 1;5) both *bath* and *blanket* are homonymous types

4.1   GOAL OF THE ANALYSIS OF HOMONYMY

The goal of the analysis of homonymy is to determine the extent to which a child's speech contains: 1) homonymous forms and 2) homonymous types, and to conclude whether the child's speech, in general, is highly homonymous in comparison to the adult language.

4.2   FORMS USED

Lexicon Sheet(s) (with homonymous forms circled from the Phonetic Analysis)

Homonymy Sheet (used for the recording of the child's homonymous forms and types)

Summary Sheet

4.3   SUMMARY OF STEPS

+--+
| Summary Box 4.   Steps in the |
| Analysis of Homonymy |
+--+
| 1. *List the homonymous forms and types that oc-|
| cur in the data* (take from the Lexicon Sheet|
| and record on the Homonymy Sheet). |
| 2. *Calculate the Proportion of Homonymous* |
| *Forms* (on Homonymy Sheet and enter on Sum-|
| mary Sheet). |
| 3. *Calculate the Proportion of Homonymous* |
| *Types* (on Homonymy Sheet and enter on Sum-|
| mary Sheet). |
| 4. *Decide the extent of homonymy.* |
+--+

4.4 PROCEDURES FOR THE ANALYSIS OF HOMONYMY

Whether or not children produce homonymy has never been in doubt, but the extent to which they do has been one of interest in studies on both normal (e.g., Ingram, 1974) and language-delayed children (c.f., Ingram, 1976). To date, however, no one has developed an effective measure to be used for comparative purposes to resolve this issue. Below, a measure is described that will help provide insight into the extent of a child's homonymy, and I hope with future research to provide normative data that can be used to decide if a particular child's use of homonymy is excessive.

The following procedures determine the extent to which a child's speech shows homonymous forms and types. The procedures are particularly useful to those who wish to look more closely at homonymy, for example, to language clinicians who attempt to eliminate it from a child's speech.

Step 1:   List the child's homonymous forms and types

These can be taken from the Lexicon Sheet on which the homonymous forms are listed. They are encircled on the Lexicon Sheet.

1. Starting from the far left column on the Lexicon Sheet, enter each phonetic form that is circled into the empty brackets on the Homonymy Sheet; enter its lexical type next to it. For example, if the Lexicon Sheet has the following entry:

dog	[dↄ]

it is entered on the Homonymy Sheet as:

Homonymous forms   Homonymous types

[dↄ]   dog

If a homonymous form has already been entered on the Homonymy Sheet, then only add its lexical type. In the above example, if we later find "call" [dↄ] , we just enter "call," which gives us:

Homonymous forms   Homonymous types

1. [dↄ]   dog, call

3. Continue through the columns of the Lexical Sheet until all homonymous forms and types have been entered.
4. If a word has more than one homonymous form, circle its second entry under homonymous types and do not count it twice. For example, if "dog" is [dↄ] and [dↄk] on the Lexicon Sheet, enter it on the Homonymy Sheet as follows:

Homonymous forms	Homonymous types	No. of types
[dↄ]	dog, call	2
[dↄk]	(dog), stuck	1

Step 2:   Calculate the Proportion of Homonymous Forms

1. Add the number of homonymous forms in the data and enter on the Homonymy Sheet.
2. Enter the number of phonetic forms, taken from the Summary Sheet, on the Homonymy Sheet.
3. Calculate the number of nonhomonymous forms by subtracting the number of homonymous forms from the number of phonetic forms, that is,

$$\begin{array}{r} \text{no. of phonetic forms} \\ - \text{ no. of homonymous forms} \\ \hline = \text{no. of nonhomonymous forms} \end{array}$$

Enter this number on the Homonymy Sheet.

4. Determine the Ratio of Homonymous Forms. This is done by first showing the ratio of the number of nonhomonymous forms to the number of homonymous forms. Then divide the smaller of these two numbers into the larger one to reduce the proportions to 1. For example, if 20:2, we divide 20/2=10 and get 10:1, meaning that we get 10 nonhomonymous forms for every homonymous one.
5. Determine the Proportion of Homonymy by dividing the number of homonyms by the number of phonetic forms, that is,

$$\frac{\text{no. of homonymous forms}}{\text{no. of phonetic forms}} = \begin{array}{l} \text{Proportion of} \\ \text{Homonymous forms} \end{array}$$

In the above example, this would give:

$$\frac{2}{22} = 0.09$$

Step 3:   Calculate the Proportion of Homonymous Types

This is done in the same way as that explained above except that the number of homonymous types, as counted on the Homonymy Sheet, and the number of lexical types, from the Summary Sheet, are used for the calculations. Then, calculate, in the same way as that noted above, a Ratio of Homonymous Types and a Proportion of Homonymous Types.

Step 4:   Enter the two Ratios and Proportions for the extent of homonymous forms and types onto the Summary Sheet

These provide an idea of the degree of homonymy in the child's data.

After these four steps are completed, one of the following conditions may be revealed from the data:

1) low degree of homonymy in both forms and types; 2) low degree of homonymy in forms, but higher in types; or 3) high degree of homonymy in forms and types.

The first condition is one in which a child's data show little homonymy. In this case, the child is efficiently using speech sounds to keep words distinct from each other. The second condition indicates that a small number of homonymous forms exist, but they represent a large number of lexical types. This is the case in an analysis conducted by Velten (1943). The author's daughter, Joan, did not have many homonymous forms, but those that did occur represented a large number of different words. The third condition is one in which a child has a lot of homonymous forms and types. In this case, individual homonymous forms do not represent a large number of lexical types and the child is not efficient in using speech sounds to keep words separate, yet he or she does not have preferred forms that have widespread use.

The important unresolved issue is determining what are "low" and "high" degrees of homonymy. The measures described here were just recently developed, therefore, norms on them do not yet exist. A preliminary report on data from several children currently being analyzed is discussed in Chapter 7. The examples of analysis provided in section 4.5 are from children who have various degrees of homonymy in forms and types, and their measures of homonymy can be used initially for comparative purposes.

4.5 SOME SAMPLES OF THE ANALYSIS OF HOMONYMY

4.5.1 Jennika 1;5

The first sample analyzed here is that of Jennika at age 1;5, and it is based on the Phonetic Analysis presented in Chapter 3, section 3.5. To follow the discussion, refer to Lexicon Sheet 2 (in Chapter 3, page 31), which shows the homonymous forms encircled.

In Step 1, we take the homonymous forms and types from the Lexicon Sheet and enter them on the Homonymy Sheet. This is a simple process because the homonymous forms have already been circled on the Lexicon Sheet (step 1, 2. (g) of the Phonetic Analysis). For Jennika, the first form circled on the Lexicon Sheet is [bat], which is entered on the Homonymy Sheet (refer to Sample Analysis 4.1 in this Chapter) under "Homonymous forms." Its lexical type, "bath" is entered under "Homonymous types." The next phonetic form circled is [bat], which has already been recorded. The new homonymous

type, "blanket," is put next to "bath" because they are both represented by the same phonetic form. The second phonetic form in the data is [aɪ] and its homonymous types are "eye" and "hi." The only other homonymous form in the data is [wa] with its lexical types being "ring-rosy" and "rock." The data on the Homonymy Sheet, after Step 1 has been completed, will look like this:

Homonymous forms   Homonymous types

1. [bat] bath, blanket
2. [aɪ] eye, hi
3. [wa] ring-rosy, rock

In Steps 2 and 3, calculate the extent of homonymy in the data in terms of homonymous forms and types, respectively. The substeps for Step 2 are completed as follows:

1. There are 3 homonymous forms for Jennika. Enter this number on the Homonymy Sheet and label that entry *(A)*.
2. Based on the Summary Sheet for Jennika, there were 70 phonetic forms. That number is entered in the space provided for total number of phonetic forms, which is then labeled *B*.
3. The number of nonhomonymous forms is determined when the number of homonymous forms is subtracted from the number of phonetic forms (or B−A). In this case, 3 from 70 leaves 67, and this entry is labeled *C*.
4. The Ratio of Homonymous Forms is a simple measure of the proportion of nonhomonymous to homonymous forms. This is shown on the Homonymy Sheet as *C:A*, indicating that the entries labeled *C* and *A* constitute this ratio. For Jennika, these are 67 and 3, respectively. To reduce the ratio to one, the smaller number is divided into the larger one. Here, 3 is divided into 67, which yields 22.
   This means that for every homonymous form there are 22 nonhomonymous ones. As is shown below, this constitutes a low degree of homonymy.
5. The measure of Proportion of Homonymous forms is obtained by dividing the number of homonymous forms (A) by the number of phonetic forms (B). Here, these numbers are 3 and 70, respectively, and yield a proportion of 0.04.

In Step 3, follow the substeps in Step 2 except that you will substitute homonymous types for homonymous forms. The number of homonymous types is obtained by adding those listed on the Homonymy Sheet. To assist in this calculation, a column for subtotals is given at the extreme right of the page because some phonetic forms may have several homonymous types. For Jennika, there are six homonymous types.

From the Summary Sheet on Jennika (or the Lexicon Sheet), we find that there are 42 lexical types. Last, there are 36 nonhomonymous types, as determined by subtracting the number of homonymous types, 6(D), from the number of lexical types, 42(E). These are entered and labeled *D, E,* and *F* to distinguish them from the first forms.

The Ratio of Homonymous types can now be calculated by dividing 36 by 6 to get 6:1. This means that there are six nonhomonymous types for every one homonymous one. The Proportion of Homonymous types will be 42(E) divided into 6(D), or 0.14. Sample Analysis 4.1 is a final representation of these three steps.

In Step 4, the calculations made at the bottom of the Homonymy Sheet are entered onto the Summary Sheet. For Jennika, these calculations are shown on the Summary Sheet as follows:

Analysis of Homonymy

| Ratio of Homonymous forms | 22:1 | Homonymous types | 6:1 |
| Proportion of Homonymous forms | 0.04 | Homonymous types | 0.14 |

Next, we need to decide whether these calculations indicate the child is Type 1, 2, or 3, as described in Step 4 of section 4.4.1. Although definitive ranges require additional research, Jennika seems to be Type 1, that is, low in the use of homonymous forms and types. This will be more evident after you see the Analyses of Homonymy presented below for two other children.

4.5.2 Joan Velten (1;10)

Velten's daughter, Joan, (Velten, 1943) is frequently cited as a child who showed a large degree of homonymy (e.g., Priestly, in press). Because of this, she is a prime candidate for the Analysis of Homonymy outlined above. Data for Joan at age 1;10 were extracted from Velten's description, and a Phonetic Analysis and Analysis of Homonymy were done. A partial summary of the Phonetic Analysis of these data as it would appear on the Summary Sheet is presented in Sample Analysis 4.2. Joan's vocabulary is quite large by age 1;10—175 words are represented, three times the number for Jennika at age 1;5. She also has more sounds acquired, 17, although her preference

for monosyllables results in most of these being for word initial and final positions.

Sample Analysis 4.3 presents the Analysis of Homonymy for Joan's data. There are 14 homonymous forms in the data for a Ratio of Homonymous forms of 9:1, as compared to Jennika's 22:1. While Joan's ratio is twice as high, the striking difference is in the Ratio of Homonymous types—Joan's is 2:1, or over three times the rate of Jennika's (6:1). Based on data analyzed in Chapter 7, it is suggested that Jennika's use of homonymous forms is unusually low, and that Joan's use of these is within the normal range. What distinguishes Joan's data is the excessive use of homonymous types, by and large the result of widespread use of the phonetic forms [bat], [bu], and [but]. She constitutes an example of a Type II child—one who uses a low or normal degree of homonymous forms but a high number of homonymous types.

4.5.3 W (1;7–1;8)

Children usually demonstrate the most extensive homonymy in the first months of word use when a few phonetic forms will represent a diversity of words. This is the case with the next and last child to be discussed, W, whose language at age 1;7–1;8 is described in an unpublished diary by his father. Using the guidelines from Chapter 2, I put these data into a broad transcription onto a Lexicon Sheet, shown here as Lexicon Sheet 4.

W has only acquired 24 words and is obviously at the very beginning of his phonological development. Using 2 as his Criterion of Frequency (the minimum possible according to Chapter 3), W's Phonetic Inventory is as follows:

Phonetic Analysis   Articulation Score _12_

Total Number of Sounds _____5_____   Criterion of Frequency _____ ($\overline{2}$ = $\overline{25}$)

word initial _____4_____   word medial _____1_____   word final _____0_____

p*   k**   kw   k
         h

Only five sounds across the three-word positions reach criterion, a demonstration of the limited ability to use diverse speech sounds. This, in turn, leads to a large degree of homonymy, as shown on W's Analysis of Homonymy, Sample Analysis 4.4. The Ratio of Homonymous forms and types are both extremely high, 3:1 and 1:2, respectively. When compared to the ratios and proportions of Joan, we see that they are even higher than her's, especially the use of homonymous forms. W typifies the Type III child hypothesized above, who uses a high degree of both homonymous forms and types. In fact, of 35 children analyzed to date using this method, W shows the most homonymy.

4.6 PRACTICE DATA

The three children who have been discussed for their use of homonymy, Jennika, Joan, and W, were all considered normal in their development. In section 3.5, on Lexicon Sheet 3, data were given from a language-delayed child, R, for the purpose of a Phonetic Analysis. Such an analysis is provided in Appendix C. On Lexicon Sheet 3 on page 55, homonymous types are circled. Use it to do an Analysis of Homonymy, using the blank Homonymy Sheet provided here and labeled *Practice Page 4.1*. When finished, compare your results with the analysis for the same data in Appendix D. How does R compare with Jennika, Joan, and W in terms of his use of homonymy? Appendix D provides a brief discussion on this point.

Child's name and age _Jennika 1;5_

Homonymous forms	Homonymous types	No. of types
1. [bat]	bath, blanket	2
2. [aɪ]	eye, hi	2
3. [wa]	ring rosy , rock	2
4. [ ]		
5. [ ]		
6. [ ]		
7. [ ]		
8. [ ]		
9. [ ]		
10. [ ]		
11. [ ]		
12. [ ]		
13. [ ]		
14. [ ]		
15. [ ]		

Summary of data

_3_ total number of homonymous forms (A)

_6_ number of homonymous types (D)

_70_ total number of phonetic forms (B)

_42_ number of lexical types (E)

_67_ total number of nonhomonymous forms (C)

_36_ number of nonhomonymous types (F)

Calculation of Extent of Homonymy

1. Ratio of Homonymous forms
   C:A _67_ : _3_   _22_ :1

2. Ratio of Homonymous types
   F:D _36_ : _6_   _6_ :1

3. Proportion of Homonymous forms

   _0.04_

4. Proportion of Homonymous types

   _0.14_

Sample Analysis 4.2   SUMMARY SHEET

Child's name and age   Joan Velten 1;10

Sample size	lexical types: 175	phonetic types: 185	phonetic tokens: 185	phonetic forms: 139

Phonetic Analysis   Articulation Score   48

Total Number of Sounds   17 (3)   Criterion of Frequency   6   ($\frac{314}{2} = \frac{157}{25}$)

word initial   8   word medial   2 (1)   word final   7 (2)

```
   m *      n *                (m)                          p * b   (n)
   b *      d *                 b      d                            t *   (d)
   f *      z *   h *                                               ts *
   w *                                                      f *    s *    z
```

syllable types:	most frequent:	CVC (75) CVCV (16)	Proportion of:	_____ Monosyllables	_____	Closed syllables

Analysis of Homonymy

Ratio of Homonymous forms _____ :1   Homonymous types _____ :1

Proportion of Homonymous forms _____   Homonymous types _____

Substitution Analysis

	m	n	ŋ	p	b	t	d	k	g	tʃ	dʒ	f	θ	s	ʃ	v	ð	z	ʒ	w	j	r	l	h		
I			▨																▨							
A																										
F																				▨	▨			▨		

Proportion of Data _____ (/67) and Matches _____ (/) Acquired sounds _____

Phonological-Process Analysis   Number of: _____ Processes _____ Affected Segments

FINAL CONSONANT DELETION

REDUCTION OF CONSONANT CLUSTERS

SYLLABLE DELETION AND REDUPLICATION

FRONTING OF PALATALS AND VELARS

STOPPING OF FRICATIVES AND AFFRICATES

SIMPLIFICATION OF LIQUIDS AND NASALS

OTHER PROCESSES

0.0–0.20	0.21–0.49	0.50–0.79	0.80–.100

Child's name and age _Joan 1;10_____

Homonymous forms	Homonymous types	No. of types
1. [bat]	bought, buckle, button, pocket, spot bad, bark, bent, bite, black, pat, block	12
2. [bu]	bowl, boy, pea, pear ball, bare, bear, beer, blow, blue	10
3. [but]	bread, break, brick, pig, put, bead, bed, bird, board, boat, boot	11
4. [dawa]	cover, tower	2
5. [dap]	cup, grandpa	2
6. [dus]	dress, pig	2
7. [hat]	hat, hot	2
8. [hus]	horse, hose	2
9. [zat]	light, shut	2
10. [zua]	little, liver	2
11. [nu]	nail, near, new, no	4
12. [nudu]	naked, noodle	2
13. [zu]	shoe, sole	2
14. [fat]	what, who	2
15. [ ]		

Summary of data

_14_ total number of homonymous forms (A)

_56_ number of homonymous types (D)

_144_ total number of phonetic forms (B)

_175_ number of lexical types (E)

_130_ total number of nonhomonymous forms (C)

_119_ number of nonhomonymous types (F)

Calculation of Extent of Homonymy

1. Ratio of Homonymous forms
   C:A _130_ : _14_   _9_ :1

2. Ratio of Homonymous types
   F:D _119_ : _56_   _2_ :1

3. Proportion of Homonymous forms
   _0.10_

4. Proportion of Homonymous types
   _0.32_

LEXICON SHEET 4

Child's name and age   W   1;7 − 1;8

types		types		types		types	
lexical	phonetic	lexical	phonetic	lexical	phonetic	lexical	phonetic
1. bang	(ka) (3x)	23. squirrel	(ka)				
2. bath	pa		ki				
3. bee	pe		kwi				
4. bike	(pa)		ke				
5. bird	pa		kwe				
	(pa)		kway				
	(pe)		kay				
6. block	(ka)	24. tata	tata				
	kwa						
7. bottle	(pa)						
8. box	(pa)						
9. bye bye	(papa)						
10. car	(ka)						
	kay						
11. clock	(ka)						
12. cracker	kwa kwa						
	kwakwa						
	kaka						
13. dog	kak (2x)						
	gavok						
14. girl	(ka)						
15. hi	hay						
16. hot	(ha)						
	(ha?)						
17. huh	(ha)						
	(ha?)						
18. kitty	kiki						
19. mama	mama(2x)						
20. nana	nana						
21. papa	(papa)						
22. plane	pwi						

HOMONYMY SHEET

Child's name and age ___W___ ___1;7 - 1;8___

Homonymous forms	Homonymous types	No. of types
1. [ka]	bank, block, car, clock	4
2. [pa]	bath, bike, bird, bottle, box	5
3. [pe]	bee, (bird)	1
4. [papa]	bye bye, papa	2
5. [kə]	girl, squirrel	2
6. [ha]	hot, huh	2
7. [haʔ]	(hot)(huh)	0
8. [ ]		
9. [ ]		
10. [ ]		
11. [ ]		
12. [ ]		
13. [ ]		
14. [ ]		
15. [ ]		

Summary of data

___7___ total number of homonymous forms (A)   ___16___ number of homonymous types (D)

___27___ total number of phonetic forms (B)   ___24___ number of lexical types (E)

___20___ total number of nonhomonymous forms (C)   ___8___ number of nonhomonymous types (F)

Calculation of Extent of Homonymy

1. Ratio of Homonymous forms
   C:A ___20___ : ___7___   ___3___ :1

2. Ratio of Homonymous types
   F:D ___8___ : ___16___   ___1___ :2

3. Proportion of Homonymous forms
   0.26

4. Proportion of Homonymous types
   0.67

Child's name and age ___R 3;11___

types		types		types		types	
lexical	phonetic	lexical	phonetic	lexical	phonetic	lexical	phonetic
1. apple	hæpo	29. duck	gʌk	55. moon	mu	83. waffle	pafo
2. arm	(nan)	30. elephant	tʌtʌt	56. one	wʌn	84. water	(dʌdo)
3. baby	bebi	31. feet	(pat)	57. paper	peto	85. web	wɛp
	bebe	32. fire	(ha)	58. pear	(peo)	86. whale	weo
4. ball	po	33. fireman	hanan	59. pie	paɪ	87. wheel	heo
5. banana	nænʌ	34. fish	pʌsə	60. robe	wop	88. whistle	pɛsɪf
6. basket	sʌkə (2x)	35. flower	(ha)	61. rock	wak	89. window	(dʌdo)
7. bathtub	bʌfʌt	36. foot	(pat)	62. safe	fef	90. witch	wɪtʃ
8. bear	(peo)	37. fork	pak	63. seagull	sigo		
9. bed	tʌt	38. hammer	næno	64. seed	sit		
10. bee	bi	39. hand	(nan)	65. shoe	suwə		
11. belt	(tap)	40. hat	hat (2x)		sup		
12. bird	bo	41. high	haɪ	66. shovel	tʌbo		
13. boat	(tap)	42. horsie	hɔrsi	67. slide	taɪ		
14. book	bʌk		sɔrsi	68. snake	sek		
15. boy	pɔɪ		sʌsi	69. spider	(dʌdo)		
16. broom	num	43. house	haʊs	70. star	da		
17. brush	bʌs	44. king	kin	71. stick	(sʌk)		
18. butter	(dʌdo)		kɪn	72. stove	dov		
19. candy	dægi	45. kitty cat	kitat	73. table	tebo		
20. comb	kom	46. ladder	dado	74. tail	tejo		
21. cow	daʊ	47. letter	tato	75. tea	ti		
22. cup	(pat)	48. light	taɪt	76. teeth	tʌf		
23. desk	(sʌk)		daɪt	77. telephone	tʌpo		
24. doctor	gaga	49. man	næn	78. tent	(tat)		
25. dog	kak (2x)		(han)	79. too	to		
	dɔk	50. marble	babo	80. top	(tat)		
	gak	51. meat	mit		(pat)		
26. door	do	52. milk	naʊk	81. towel	taʊ		
27. dress	sæs	53. mommy	mami (2x)		tajo		
28. drum	lam	54. momma	mama	82. tractor	gago		

HOMONYMY SHEET

Child's name and age   R   3;11

Homonymous forms	Homonymous types	No. of types
1. [ ]	_____	_____
2. [ ]	_____	_____
3. [ ]	_____	_____
4. [ ]	_____	_____
5. [ ]	_____	_____
6. [ ]	_____	_____
7. [ ]	_____	_____
8. [ ]	_____	_____
9. [ ]	_____	_____
10. [ ]	_____	_____
11. [ ]	_____	_____
12. [ ]	_____	_____
13. [ ]	_____	_____
14. [ ]	_____	_____
15. [ ]	_____	_____

Summary of data

_____ total number of homonymous forms (A)   _____ number of homonymous types (D)

_____ total number of phonetic forms (B)   _____ number of lexical types (E)

_____ total number of nonhomonymous forms (C)   _____ number of nonhomonymous types (F)

Calculation of Extent of Homonymy

1. Ratio of Homonymous forms
   C:A _____ : _____   _____ :1

2. Ratio of Homonymous types
   F:D _____ : _____   _____ :1

3. Proportion of Homonymous forms

   _____

4. Proportion of Homonymous types

   _____

CHAPTER 5

Substitution Analysis

Glossary of Basic Terms

The following are some typical adult words attempted by children:

"to/mato"   "candle"   "pig"   "paper"
"bath/tub"   "pencil"   "cow"

(The shills represent syllable boundaries that were placed according to the rules explained below.)

initial (or prevocalic) consonant(s): a consonant or consonant cluster that appears before a vowel: 1) at the beginning of a word, e.g., [p] in "pig," "pencil"; or 2) after a syllable boundary, e.g., [m] in "to/mato" and [t] in "bath/tub."

final (or postvocalic) consonant(s): a consonant or consonant cluster that occurs after a vowel: 1) at the end of a word, e.g., [g] in "pig," [b] in "bath/tub"; or 2) before a syllable boundary, e.g., [θ] in "bath/tub."

ambisyllabic (intervocalic) consonant(s): a consonant or consonant cluster that occurs between two vowels or syllabic segments and functions both to end one syllable and to begin the next, e.g., [p] in "paper," [nd] in "candle," and [ns] in "pencil."

5.1 GOAL OF SUBSTITUTION ANALYSIS

The goal of this type of analysis is to determine the substitutions used by the child in his or her attempts to produce the initial, final, and ambisyllabic consonants and clusters of the adult language.

5.2 FORMS USED

Lexicon Sheet (from which data is taken)
Three Consonant Inventory Sheets—Lexical Types
Item and Replica Sheet
Summary Sheet

5.3 SUMMARY OF STEPS

Summary Box 5. Steps in Substitution Analysis

1. *Isolate syllables of adult words*—do this on Lexicon Sheet to determine initial, final, and ambisyllabic segments
2. *Record adult words and sounds attempted*—enter separately for initial, final, and ambisyllabic segments on Consonant Inventory Sheets—Lexical Types
3. *Enter child's substitutes for adult sounds*—record above adult words on Consonant Inventory Sheets
4. *Determine frequency of substitutions*—record on right half of Item and Replica Sheet
5. *Summarize most frequent substitutions*—enter on Summary Sheet
6. *Calculate degree of substitution*—enter on Summary Sheet

5.4 DISCUSSION OF PROCEDURES

Substitution analysis is probably the most commonly used analytic procedure in phonological studies. Despite this, methods vary greatly from study to study concerning both what is counted and why something is counted. Accordingly, there are no shared criteria on how substitutions are recorded and counted. One of the most avoided issues has been the question of syllable boundaries. In other words, what do we mean when we refer to initial, medial, and final substitutions? The Glossary of Basic Terms (above) introduces the way this is done here, and Step 1 describes in detail the determination of syllable boundaries.

Step 1: Isolate syllables of adult words

On the Lexicon Sheet, draw a vertical line in red between the syllables of multisyllable adult words attempted, using the following rules:

1. Place a syllable boundary after an unstressed syllable preceding a stressed syllable, e.g., banana= ba/nana; telephone=tele/phone.
2. Place a syllable boundary between consonants or between a vowel and a consonant if both syllables carry stress, that is, if the word is a compound, e.g., "sunset"="sun/set" as opposed to "pencil"="pencil," or "drive-in"="drive/in" as opposed to "driving"="driving."
3. Place a syllable boundary between consonants that occur between syllabic segments if those consonants cannot occur as permissable word final clusters in English, e.g., "napkin"="nap/kin," "chimney"="chim/ney" because [pk] and [mn] are not permissable final clusters.
   Note: all nasal and stop sequences are considered permissable final clusters even though some never occur, e.g., [mb], [ŋg].
4. All other consonants between vowels are considered ambisyllabic (or intervocalic).

After syllable boundaries are placed, it is possible to locate all of the initial, final, and ambisyllabic consonants in adult words, as described in the Glossary of Basic Terms. These then constitute the target sounds for the child. The next step is to organize these sounds for the substitution analysis, as is exemplified in Sample Analyses 5.1, 5.2, and 5.3.

Step 2: Record adult words and sounds attempted

1. Label a Consonant Inventory Sheet—Lexical Types *Initial Consonants* by placing a check in the blank space for "initial."
2. Place lexical types from the Lexicon Sheet into boxes according to their syllable initial sounds. If the adult model is produced correctly by the child, enter only the number of the lexical item on the Lexicon Sheet. These are put into the far left column. If the child does not correctly produce the

adult sound, enter the word itself, using the following suggested guidelines:
a. Put monosyllables in center column.
b. Place multisyllabic words in far right column.

Example

These guidelines may need to be varied, however, according to the number of words attempted, space, etc.

c. Clusters are cross-listed. After placing a cluster in the box of its first consonant, e.g., "plane" above, place it in the box (or boxes) of its other consonant or consonants. In the above example with /pl/ clusters, we might also have

d. When the initial consonant does not begin the word, be sure to show the appropriate syllable boundary, e.g., "po/tato" can go into the /p/ box as "potato," but in the /t/ box as "po/tato."
e. When the number of correct lexical types exceeds five (i.e., the space allowed in the box), either 1) continue listing numbers on the back of the sheet, or 2) circle fifth number to indicate that other correct entries occur but are not entered, for example,

Method 2 is a time-saving alternative that allows us to avoid entering all of a child's words in case the sound has been acquired. Its use is sufficient in most cases and it will be used in the analysis presented below.

f. If a lexical type occurs twice, e.g., once singly and once in isolation, e.g., "12. cat" [kæt], "13. catfood" [kætfud], only one entry is made if the consonant is the same in both. In this example, only 12 would be entered in the box for initial /k/.

g. If a lexical type has two or more phonetic types, one of which is correct and the other(s) of which shows substitutes, it is entered twice, once as correct, and once in its full form. For example, 13. "cat" [kæ] [tæ] would be entered:

/k/	13	cat	

3. Repeat procedure for ambisyllabic consonants, using a Consonant Inventory Sheet—Lexical Types labeled *ambisyllabic consonants.*
4. Repeat procedure for final consonants, using a Consonant Inventory Sheet—Lexical Types labeled "final consonants."
   Note: enter syllabic consonants, e.g., "bottle" and "paper" in separate /l/ and /r/ boxes, respectively.

After Step 2, all of the adult words that were produced with mismatches are organized and ready for the substitution analysis. The placement of the data into this format is also organized in a way that would allow a phonological process analysis to be done if one is desired (c.f., Chapter 6). This organization eliminates the need to search randomly through the Lexicon Sheet for adult target sounds.

Step 3: **Enter child's substitutes for adult sounds**

Note: the order of entering the substitutes is not fixed—it is up to the individual analyst. The one presented here is one that simply follows the top row and

1. Enter the substitutes on the Consonant Inventory Sheet labeled Lexical Types—*Initial Consonants.* Begin by taking the top left box on the sheet and enter the substitutes by finding each word on the Lexicon Sheet and recording its substitute, using the following guidelines:
   a. All substitutes are entered in red directly above the sound attempted, e.g., "man" [dæ], "match" [baɫ], "monkey" [baki] would be shown as

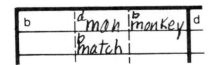

   b. If a sound is deleted, enter "Ø," e.g., "cow" [aʊ] would be entered

   Ø
   cow

   c. If a syllable is deleted, indicate this with a dash, e.g., "banana" [nænə] for /b/ would be
   "‾banana"
   d. If there are several phonetic types (or tokens) all having the same substitute, simply enter the substitute once, e.g., "dog" [ga] [gag] [gak] for /d/ would be entered

   g
   dog.

e. If there is more than one substitute, enter each one once. For example, dog [ga] [gag] [gak] [da] for /d/ would be entered

   g d
   dog.

f. If there is a cluster, show its substitute according to the box it is in, e.g., "cloud" [ka] would be shown

   k
   cloud

   in the /k/ box, and

   ∅
   cloud

   in the /l/ box.
g. There will be some cases, usually with clusters, in which it is not always clear for what the target sound is being substituted. For example, in [sæs] for "dress," the initial [s] could be considered as a substitute for either /d-/ or /r/, with the other being deleted. The following guidelines are offered to help in such cases. These are cases in which the syllable structure of the child's word is not the same as that of the adult's word.
   i. When the child's word has fewer syllables than that of the adult word, line the words up by matching the vowels, e.g., [nænʌ] [nʌnæ] and [bænʌ] for "banana" would be lined up as follows:

   banana   banana   banana
    | | | | | |
   nænʌ   nʌnæ   bænʌ

   In this case initial [n] is a correct match in the first example, and a substitute for /b/ in the second. In the third example, [b] is a substitute for initial /n/.
   ii. If two or more consonants in the adult word are reduced in the child's, consider the child's sound as a substitute for the adult sound that matches in the feature obstruent versus sonorant, e.g., in [sæs] for "dress," [s] initial is a substitute for /d-/ because they both are obstruents. In [lʌm] for "drum," however, [l] is for /r/, and /d-/ will be considered deleted. If both target sounds are obstruent or sonorant, then consider the child's sound a substitute for

the adult sound that agrees with it in manner of articulation, e.g., in [te] for "skate," both /s/ and /k/ are obstruents. Because [t] is a stop, however, it is considered as a substitute for /k/.

If the child's sound cannot be matched to one of the adult target sounds in terms of sonorance, obstruence, or manner, then use place of articulation to decide, for example, if [pɪs] occurs for "picked," the final [-s] replaces /-t/ because it matches it in place of articulation. If place is not the same for the child's sound and any of the adult ones, then consider the child's sound as a substitute for the adult sound that is least marked in terms of position on the following scale of markedness: alveolar > labial > velar > palato-alveolar, e.g, in [pɪp] for "picked," the final [-p] would be considered a substitute for [-t] because the alveolar position is less marked than the velar one.

The decision matrix described above can be summarized as follows:

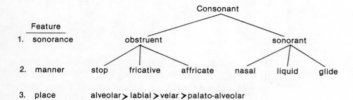

2. Repeat steps for ambisyllabic consonants. If a consonant has no substitute because a syllable has been dropped, indicate this with a dash, e.g., "butter" [bʌt] would be entered: but̲t̲e̲r̲. Do not count later as a substitute.

3. Repeat steps for final consonants. If a consonant has no substitute because a vowel has been added, enter V, e.g., "duck" [dʌki] for final /-k/ would be entered: duck^V. Do not count it later as a substitute. Note that separate boxes are used for syllabic /-l/ and /-r/.

As you do the substitutes for each adult target sound, it becomes clear which sounds are being produced correctly and which have patterns of replacement. The next step is to record this information by summarizing the main patterns and eliminating infrequent ones (c.f., Sample Analysis 5.4).

Step 4: **Determine frequency of substitutions**

The child's frequent substitutes are to be entered on the diagrams on the right side of the Item and Replica Sheet. The blank boxes in the diagrams on the right are used for showing the sounds produced by the child for the adult models shown in the corresponding box in the diagram on the left. For example, the top left box has an /m/ inside, which represents adult sounds with initial /m/s. In the corresponding blank box on the right, show what the child substitutes for /m/.

1.
   a. Take, from the Consonant Inventory Sheet labeled lexical types—*initial consonants,* the substitutes produced at least twice for each adult sound and enter them into the appropriate box. Indicate their frequency.

   Example

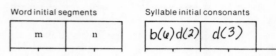

This shows that the child used 6 lexical types with a [b] substitute and 2 with a [d] substitute for adult /m/. For adult /n/, 3 lexical types had [d].

   b. If no substitutes occur at least twice, and at least two words show correct production, place a check (✓) in the box. Otherwise, also enter the number of correct productions, if there are two or more, as optional information.
   c. Deletions are entered as Ø and with their frequency.
   d. If a dash occurs to show a syllable has been deleted, then nothing is counted for that occurrence.
   e. If there are no attempts at an adult target, or if no sound occurs more than once, then place a dash in the box to indicate no data.
2. Repeat steps for ambisyllabic consonants.
3. Repeat steps for final consonants.

Step 4 reduces all the substitution data to the Item and Replica Sheet. Along with the data from the Phonetic Analysis, this Sheet becomes a complete summary of the child's segmental abilities. The next step is to summarize these data onto the Summary Sheet (c.f., Sample Analysis 5.5).

Step 5: **Summarize most frequent substitutions**

The Summary Sheet contains a display of the major consonants in English along with I, A, F rows to indicate Initial, Ambisyllabic, and Final syllable positions.
1. Enter the substitutes from the Item and Replica Sheet for each of the sounds and their word positions.
   a. Do not transfer information on frequency.
   b. If more than two substitutes occur, only enter the two most frequent ones.
   c. If the only sound produced by the child matches the adult model, enter a check in the box to indicate correctness, or a match.
   d. Enter a dash if there is no data on a sound.
   e. Combine the summary for final syllabic and nonsyllabic /-r/ and /-l/ onto the Summary Sheet.
2. Circle in red where the mismatches occur. These will need to be explained by later phonological process analysis.

The last step in the Substitution Analysis represents an attempt to develop some measures for quantifying the results obtained. These have been developed in the hope that they will eventually lead to useful measures for comparisons of the child's performance over time.

Step 6: **Measuring the extent of substitution**

To get an idea of the child's ability to match the adult models, it is possible to calculate the extent to which matches occur. The measure described below is a first attempt to develop a way to quantify this ability.

1. The first step is to determine the number and proportion of matches for each syllable position. There are 22, 24, and 21 potential matches for initial, intervocalic, and final consonants, respectively, as can be determined from the number of squares on the Summary Sheet under the Substitution Analysis.
   a. Count the number of matches for each syllable position and enter this over the total number of adult sounds attempted by the child, placed to the right of the Substitution Analysis. Example:

Substitution Analysis

   b. Calculate the proportion of matches for each syllable position by dividing the number of matches by the number of sounds attempted (see above example).
2. Calculate the total number of matches and sounds attempted, and the Proportion of Matches. These are entered on the Summary Sheet in the appropriate spaces. Example

Proportion of Data _____ (/) and Matches __0.14__ (4/28)

This means that this child is only matching the adult sound 14% of the time.

3. Because this Proportion of Matches may vary according to the number of sounds attempted, it is useful also to calculate the Proportion of Data. This is the number of consonants attempted over the total number of possible words, which for American English is 67. Example

Proportion of Data __0.42__ (28/67)

A typical language sample will yield data on approximately 50% of the possible adult sounds produced.

4. Count the number of sounds acquired. These are the sounds that have checks in all possible syllable positions. Enter this figure in the appropriate place on the Summary Sheet. Example

Acquired sounds __0__

Some normative data on these measures is provided in Chapter 7.

5.5 SAMPLE SUBSTITUTION ANALYSIS

The first sample analysis is done on the data for Jennika at age 1;5, as shown on Lexicon Sheet 2 (p. 64). These data have already been treated in the Phonetic Analysis and the Analysis of Homonymy. Follow the steps in section 5.4 along with the discussion below.

In Step 1, divide the multisyllabic words attempted by the child into their various syllables by placing syllable boundaries on the Lexicon Sheet. In Jennika's data, the following multisyllabic words occur:

alldone	daddy	mommy
apple	get down	ring rosy
blanket	ice-cream	sweater
bye-bye	kitty	water
cookie	Kristen	

Rule 1 in Step 1 does not apply because there are no stressed syllables preceded by unstressed syllables, such as "banana," "potato." Rule 2 places a boundary between compounds and applies in the following words:

all/done	ring/rosy
get/down	bye/bye
ice/cream	

The remaining words have initial stress followed by an unstressed syllable, indicating ambisyllabic segments. Two of these have clusters, "blanket" and "Kristen." Both /ŋk/ and /st/ may occur as permissible final English clusters, so neither of them is split by a syllable boundary by Rule 3. For Jennika, Rule 3. does not apply at all. Note that these syllable boundaries have already been made on Lexicon Sheet 2.

In Step 2, place the adult words from the Lexicon Sheet onto Consonant Inventory Sheets. Initial segments are entered first, so label a Consonant Inventory Sheet—Lexical Types by placing a check mark in the blank for initial segments (c.f., Sample Analysis 5.1). The first word on Jennika's Lexicon Sheet is "all/done," which contains two syllables. The first syllable correctly begins with a vowel so we place its number, 1, into the far left column of the vowel box. The second syllable correctly begins with /d/, so "1" is placed inside the far left column or the /d/ box. The next word, "apple," also goes into the vowel box, below "alldone." The next four words "bath," "bib," "bike," and "bird" all go into a /b/ box, and again only their numbers are entered because the child produced a [b] in each. The next word, "blanket," has a cluster, so it is entered into both the /b/ box (in the far left column), and also into the /l/ box. In the latter case, there are two different substitutions, therefore the entire word is written into the far right column. The rest of the words can be entered in like fashion (c.f., Sample Analysis 5.1). Because there are more than five correct words beginning with /b/, the last number entered in the /b/ box in Sample Analysis 5.1 is circled to indicate there are additional items not given. There are a couple of other entries that deserve comment. The word "down" occurs with a correct [d] in both 15, "down," and 17, "get/down," so it is only entered once (c.f., Step 2, 2.g).

The entry of the ambisyllabic segments does not take long because there are only the few words discussed above. These are "apple," "blanket," "cookie," "daddy," "kitty," "Kristen," "mommy," "sweater," "water," and the second half of "ring/rosy." The Consonant Inventory Sheet for these is given on Sample Analysis 5.2. Notice that the second part of "ring-rosy" with an intervocalic /z/ is entered with a dash because the child has dropped the last syllable and no intervocalic segment was even attempted.

The last part of Step 2 is to enter the syllable final consonants on a new Consonant Inventory Sheet. The first word, "alldone," has two syllables and therefore two final consonants, /l/ and /n/, which are placed into /l/ and /n/ boxes, respectively, in both cases in the far right column. The second word, "apple," has a final syllabic /ļ/, which is placed in a box below the /l/ box, to the far left with its number, 2, because one phonetic type is correct, and in the far right column also because the /l/ is deleted in one instance. The first word with a final cluster is "box," which has a final /ks/. It will go into both the /k/ and /s/ boxes. Sample Analysis 5.3 shows the entry of the final consonants for Jennika.

Step 3 involves entering the child's productions in red over the target sounds attempted. This is already shown for Jennika on Samples Analysis 5.1, 5.2, and 5.3. For purposes of demonstration, I will assume this has not yet been done. It would be possible to start anyplace, but let's begin with the initial segments (Sample Analysis 5.1), with the /b/ box. Because all the syllables beginning with /b/ are correct matches, nothing more needs to be done. This is also the case for /d/ and /dz/. For /g/, we have "get-down" shown, which requires, upon checking the Lexicon Sheet, a [d] shown over the /g/. The child's productions are examined until all the substitutes for the various targets are recorded. A careful examination of the Sample Analysis should show how this has taken place. After the initial substitutes are entered, the ambisyllabic and final consonants are then done.

There are few ambisyllabic segments and, subsequently, few entries necessary. For "sweater," Jennika said [waʃ] and [watʃ], neither of which contains an intervocalic consonant. In this case then, a dash is placed above "sweater" to show that a syllable has been deleted.

A similar kind of situation arises in the entries for final consonants. For final /-g/ in "dog," Jennika produced [dɔdi]. Because her form contains no final consonant, no entry can be made, except for "V," to indicate an added vowel. As can be seen on Sample Analysis 5.3, most of the final consonants are deleted and require the entry of "Ø."

We are now ready for Step 4, the summary of the frequent substitutions onto the Item and Replica Sheet. Beginning with the initial segments on Sample Analysis 5.1, we count up substitutions and enter onto the Item and Replica Sheet all those that occur at least twice. In a small sample like this, there will be a small number that even meet this minimal criterion. Starting with /b/, simply place a check in the appropriate box because all of these are correct. Checks to indicate matches (or correctness) are also entered for /p/, /d/, and /w/. In the case of /p/, there has been a substitute [b] that has occurred, but only once. Target sounds that show at least two substitutes are /k/, /s/, /r/, and /h/. Their substitutes and frequencies are entered, as shown on Sample Analysis 5.4.

For ambisyllabic consonants, most entries show only one substitute. The only target showing more than one substitute type is /k/ where two [t]s occur, one in "blanket" and one in "cookie." It is, therefore, the only entry made in summary onto the Item and Replica Sheet.

There are several substitutes that meet criterion for final consonants, as shown on Sample Analysis 5.4. Final /-n/ has four cases of [m], which are to be entered. The final alveolars /t, d, s, r, l/ all show deletion, although [t] is a productive phonetic element for Jennika (c.f., Sample Analysis 3.1). Final /k/ shows two substitutes, with [t] occurring twice and deletion three times.

These substitutes are next summarized onto the Summary Sheet in Step 5. We can do this by starting with the initial sounds and checking off those that match the adult model. This is the case for /m, p, b, d, w/, so these boxes are checked on the Summary Sheet (c.f., Sample Analysis 5.5). Next, the substitutes for /k, s, r, h/ are entered and circled in red because they show mismatches. For the ambisyllabic consonants, only /k/ needs to be entered and circled, in this case, because it is a mismatch. Last, the entries for the final consonants are made. For Jennika, there are no matches so she is obviously doing much better at the acquisition of initial sounds than of final sounds. All of the final consonant entries will be circled.

The last step is to measure the extent of substitution that occurs. First, calculate the extent of matches for each syllable position. Here, the initial position is clearly superior, with five out of nine matches, compared to no matches for either medial (0 for 1) or final (0 for 7) consonants. Overall, 0.29 of the target sounds show matching. Next, calculate the extent of the data. Out of the 67 possible sounds that can be attempted (or boxes that occur on the Summary Sheet), 17 are filled, for a proportion of 0.25. This indicates that the child is consistently attempting approximately one-fourth of all possible adult sounds. Last, because no sounds show matches in all possible positions, we can conclude that none of the English consonants have yet to be acquired (c.f. Step 6,d).

5.5 PRACTICE DATA

The sample from Jennika was a small one but at least it shows the rudiments of how a substitution analysis is done. Using the following Practice Pages, attempt your own analysis of the data from R on Lexicon Sheet 3. Appendix E, which contains representations of how the data will look when analyzed according to the Steps outlined above, should be useful to you. After each step, check the Appendix to be certain that the analysis is being done correctly. Use the following guidelines:

Step 1: do directly on Lexicon Sheet 3, page 70. (check with Appendix E, Discussion of the Analysis)

Step 2: do on Practice Pages 5.1, 5.2, and 5.3 (check with Appendices E, 3, 4, and 5)

Step 3: do on Practice Pages 5.1, 5.2, and 5.3 (check with Appendices E, 3, 4, and 5)

Step 4: do on Practice Page 5.4 (check after Appendix E, 2)

Steps 5 and 6: do on Practice Page 5.5 (after, check Appendix E, 1)

LEXICON SHEET 2

Child's name and age ___Jennika 1;5___

	types		types		types		types
lexical	phonetic	lexical	phonetic	lexical	phonetic	lexical	phonetic
1. all/done	1 ædʌm (2x)	15. down	31 daʊ	35. rock	61 (wa)		
	2 ədʌm		32 dʌm		62 wati		
2. apple	3 apʊ	16. egg	33 l	36. see	63 si (2x)		
	4 æpᴐl	17. eye	34 (aɪ)	37. shoe	64 ʃʊ (2x)		
3. bath	5 (bat)	18. get/down	35 didʌm	38. spoon	65 pʌm		
4. bib	6 bɪ	19. hat	36 atʃ (2x)	39. sweater	66 waʃ		
5. bike	7 baɪ		37 aɪtʃ		67 watʃ		
6. bird	8 bi	20. hot	38 at	40. up	68 ap (2x)		
7. blanket	9 bwa		39 ati		69 ʌp		
	10 (bat)	21. hi	40 aɪdi		70 api (2x)		
	11 bwaki		41 (aɪ) (2x)	41. walk	71 at		
	12 bwati (2x)		42 haɪ	42. water	72 wawa		
	13 bwat	22. ice/cream	43 dʒudʒʊ		73 wʌwʌ		
	14 bati	23. juice	44 dʒʊ (2x)				
8. book	15 ba (2x)		45 dʒʊs (2x)				
	16 bʌ (2x)		46 dʒʊt				
	17 baʔ	24. kitty	47 dɪti				
	18 bʊt (2x)	25. Kristen	48 dɪdɪn				
	19 bʌt	26. mommy	49 mami				
9. box	20 batʃ	27. more	50 mᴐ				
10. bye/bye	21 babaɪ		51 mo				
	22 bəbaɪ		52 mʌ				
11. chair	23 dɛ	28. mouth	53 mæt				
12. cookie	24 duti (2x)	29. no	54 no				
	25 didi (3x)	30. out	55 aʊ				
	26 dodi	31. pee	56 pipi				
	27 digi	32. poop	57 bʌbo				
	28 gigi		58 bʌbu				
13. daddy	29 dʒædi	33. ride	59 waɪ				
14. dog	30 dᴐdi	34. ring/rosy	60 (wa)				

Sample Analysis 5.1

Lexical Types   Child's name and age _Jennika 1;5_

✓ initial   _____ ambisyllabic   _____ final

b 3			d 1			dʒ 23			g		d get down
4			13									
5			14									
6			15									
⑦												
p 31	poop		t			tʃ	d chair		k		d,ʒ cookie / d,dʒ ice/cream / d kitty / d Kristen
38											
v			z			ʒ			ð		
f			s 36	ø spoon	ø sweater	ʃ 37			θ		
w 39			l		w,ø blanket	r	w ride	ø ice cream	h 21	ø hat
41							w rock	ø Kristen		ø hi
42								w ring rosy		ø hot
									vowel 1		dʒ ice cream
									2		
									16		
									17		
									30		
m 26			n 29						ŋ		
27											
28											

Sample Analysis 5.2

CONSONANT INVENTORY SHEET

Lexical Types   Child's name and age _Jennika 1;5_

_____ initial   ✓ ambisyllabic   _____ final

b			d 13			dʒ			g		
p 2			t 24	kristen sweater water	tʃ			k 7	blanket cookie	
v			z	ring rosy	ʒ			ð		
f			s	Kristen	ʃ			θ		
w			l		r			h		
								vowel		
m 26			n					ŋ	blanket	

CONSONANT INVENTORY SHEET
Lexical Types   Child's name and age Jennika 1;5

_____ initial   _____ ambisyllabic   ✓ final

b	bib^ø		d	bird^ø ride^ø		dʒ			g	dog^v egg^ø	
p 40	poop^v		t 20	hat^{tʃ} blanket^{ʔø} hot^v get/down^ø out^ø		tʃ			k	bike^ø book^{ø,ʔ,t} box^{tʃ} rock^{ø,v} walk^t	
v			z			ʒ			ð		
f			s 23	box^{tʃ} juice^{ø,t}		ʃ			θ	bath^t mouth^t	
w			l	all/done^ø		r	chair^ø more^ø		h		
				apple^u		r̃			sweater water^{ʌ,a}	vowel		
m	ice cream^ø		n 48	down^{ø,m} all done^m spoon^m					ŋ	ring, rosy	

ITEM AND REPLICA SHEET

Child's name and age *Jennika 1;5*

Child's Phonetic Inventory

Word initial segments

m		n					
p	b	t	d	tʃ	dʒ	k	g
f	v	θ	ð	ʃ			
f	v	s	z			Vowel	
w		r		j		h	
w		l		j		h	

Word medial consonants

m		n				ŋ	
p	b	t	d	tʃ	dʒ	k	g
f	v	θ	ð	ʃ	3		
f	v	s	z	ʃ	3		
w		r		j		h	
w		l		j		h	

Word final consonants

m		n				ŋ	
p	b	t	d	tʃ	dʒ	k	g
f	v	θ	ð	ʃ	3		
f	v	s	z	ʃ	3		
		r		ɾ			
		l		ḷ			

Child's Substitutions

Syllable initial consonants

✓		—					
✓	✓	—	✓	—	—	d(3)	—
—	—	—		—			
—	—	∅(2)	—				
✓		w(3) ∅(2)		—		∅(3)	
✓		—		—		∅(3)	

Ambisyllabic consonants

—		—				—	
—	—	—`	—	—	—	t(2)	—
		—		—	—		
—	—	—	—	—	—		
—		—		—			
—		—					

Syllable final consonants

—		m(3)				—	
—	—	∅(3)	∅(2)	—	—	∅(3) t(2)	—
—	—	t(2)	—	—	—		
—	—	∅(2)	—	—	—		
		∅(2)		—			
		—		—			

Sample Analysis 5.5   SUMMARY SHEET

Child's name and age _Jennika 1;5_

| Sample size | lexical types: _____ | phonetic types: _____ | phonetic tokens: _____ | phonetic forms: _____ |

<u>Phonetic Analysis</u> Articulation Score _____
Total Number of Sounds _____ Criterion of Frequency _____ ($\overline{2}$ = $\overline{25}$)
word initial _____ word medial _____ word final _____

syllable types: most frequent: _____ Proportion of: _____ Monosyllables _____ Closed syllables

<u>Analysis of Homonymy</u>
Ratio of Homonymous forms _____:1 Homonymous types _____:1
Proportion of Homonymous forms _____ Homonymous types _____

<u>Substitution Analysis</u>

	m	n	ŋ	p	b	t	d	k	g	tʃ	dʒ	f	θ	s	ʃ	v	ð	z	ʒ	w	j	r	l	h	
I	✓		▨	✓	✓		✓	⊘						⊘					▨	✓		ⓦ/⊘		⊘	0.56(5/9)
A								⊕																	0.00(0/1)
F		ⓜ				⊘	⊘	⊘/⊕					⊕	⊘					▨			⊘		▨	0.00(0/7)

Proportion of Data _0.25_____ (17/67) and Matches _0.29_____ (5/17) Acquired sounds _____0____

<u>Phonological Process Analysis</u> Number of:_____Processes_____Affected Segments

FINAL CONSONANT DELETION

REDUCTION OF CONSONANT CLUSTERS

SYLLABLE DELETION AND REDUPLICATION

FRONTING OF PALATALS AND VELARS

STOPPING OF FRICATIVES AND AFFRICATES

SIMPLIFICATION OF LIQUIDS AND NASALS

OTHER PROCESSES

     0.0–0.20   0.21–0.49   0.50–0.79   0.80–.100

LEXICON SHEET 3

Child's name and age ___R 3;11___

types lexical	phonetic	types lexical	phonetic	types lexical	phonetic	types lexical	phonetic
1. apple	hæpo	29. duck	gʌk	55. moon	mu	83. waffle	pafo
2. arm	nan	30. elephant	tʌtʌt	56. one	wʌn	84. water	dʌdo
3. baby	bebi	31. feet	pat	57. paper	peto	85. web	wɛp
	bebe	32. fire	ha	58. pear	peo	86. whale	weo
4. ball	po	33. fireman	hanan	59. pie	paɪ	87. wheel	heo
5. banana	nænʌ	34. fish	pʌsə	60. robe	wop	88. whistle	pɛsɪf
6. basket	sʌkə(2x)	35. flower	ha	61. rock	wak	89. window	dʌdo
7. bathtub	bʌfʌt	36. foot	pat	62. safe	fef	90. witch	wɪtʃ
8. bear	peo	37. fork	pak	63. seagull	sigo		
9. bed	tʌt	38. hammer	næno	64. seed	sit		
10. bee	bi	39. hand	nan	65. shoe	suwə		
11. belt	tap	40. hat	hat(2x)		sup		
12. bird	bo	41. high	haɪ	66. shovel	tʌbo		
13. boat	tap	42. horsie	hɔrsi	67. slide	taɪ		
14. book	bʌk		sɔrsi	68. snake	sek		
15. boy	pɔɪ		sʌsi	69. spider	dʌdo		
16. broom	num	43. house	haʊs	70. star	da		
17. brush	bʌʃ	44. king	kin	71. stick	sʌk		
18. butter	dʌdo		kɪn	72. stove	dov		
19. candy	dægi	45. kitty cat	kitat	73. table	tebo		
20. comb	kom	46. ladder	dado	74. tail	tejo		
21. cow	daʊ	47. letter	tato	75. tea	ti		
22. cup	pat	48. light	taɪt	76. teeth	tʌf		
23. desk	sʌk		daɪt	77. telephone	tʌpo		
24. doctor	gaga	49. man	næn	78. tent	tat		
25. dog	kak(2x)		nan	79. too	to		
	dɔk	50. marble	babo	80. top	tat		
	gak	51. meat	mit		pat		
26. door	do	52. milk	naʊk	81. towel	taʊ		
27. dress	sæs	53. mommy	mami(2x)		tajo		
28. drum	lam	54. momma	mama	82. tractor	gago		

Practice Page 5.1

CONSONANT INVENTORY SHEET
Lexical Types   Child's name and age ___R 3; 11___

✓ initial   _____ ambisyllabic   _____ final

b			d			dʒ			g		
p			**t**			**tʃ**			**k**		
v			**z**			**ʒ**			**ð**		
f			**s**			**ʃ**			**θ**		
w			**l**			**r**			**h**		
									vowel		
m			**n**						**ŋ**		

CONSONANT INVENTORY SHEET

Lexical Types   Child's name and age ___R__3;11_____

_____ initial   ✓ ambisyllabic   _____ final

b			d			dʒ			g		
p			**t**			**tʃ**			**k**		
v			**z**			**ʒ**			**ð**		
f			**s**			**ʃ**			**θ**		
w			**l**			**r**			**h**		
									vowel		
m			**n**						**ŋ**		

CONSONANT INVENTORY SHEET

Lexical Types   Child's name and age _R 3;11_

_____ initial   _____ ambisyllabic   ✓ final

b			d			dʒ			g		
p			t			tʃ			k		
v			z			ʒ			ð		
f			s			ʃ			θ		
w			l			r			h		
									vowel		
m			n						ŋ		

ITEM AND REPLICA SHEET

Child's name and age ___R___ 3;11___

Child's Phonetic Inventory

Word initial segments

m		n				
p	b	t	d	tʃ	dʒ	k	g
f	v	θ	ð	ʃ		
		s	z		Vowel	
w		r		j		h
		l				

Child's Substitutions

Syllable initial consonants

(empty grid)

Word medial consonants

m		n		ŋ
p	b	t	d	tʃ	dʒ	k	g
f	v	θ	ð	ʃ	3	
		s	z			
w		r		j		h
		l				

Ambisyllabic consonants

(empty grid)

Word final consonants

m		n		ŋ
p	b	t	d	tʃ	dʒ	k	g
f	v	θ	ð	ʃ	3	
		s	z			
		r		ɾ		
		l		ɭ		

Syllable final consonants

(empty grid)

SUMMARY SHEET

Child's name and age ___R 3;11___

Sample size | lexical types: _____ | phonetic types: _____ | phonetic tokens: _____ | phonetic forms: _____

Phonetic Analysis   Articulation Score _____

Total Number of Sounds _____   Criterion of Frequency _____ ($\overline{2}$ = $\overline{25}$)

word initial _____   word medial _____   word final _____

syllable types: | most frequent: _____ | Proportion of: _____ | Monosyllables _____ | Closed syllables

Analysis of Homonymy

Ratio of Homonymous forms _____:1   Homonymous types _____:1

Proportion of Homonymous forms _____   Homonymous types _____

Substitution Analysis

	m	n	ŋ	p	b	t	d	k	g	tʃ	dʒ	f	θ	s	ʃ	v	ð	z	ʒ	w	j	r	l	h		
I			▓																▓							
A																										
F																				▓	▓	▓		▓		

Proportion of Data _____ (/67) and Matches _____ (/) Acquired sounds _____

Phonological Process Analysis   Number of:_____Processes_____Affected Segments

FINAL CONSONANT DELETION

REDUCTION OF CONSONANT CLUSTERS

SYLLABLE DELETION AND REDUPLICATION

FRONTING OF PALATALS AND VELARS

STOPPING OF FRICATIVES AND AFFRICATES

SIMPLIFICATION OF LIQUIDS AND NASALS

OTHER PROCESSES

0.0–0.20	0.21–0.49	0.50–0.79	0.80–.100

CHAPTER 6

Phonological Process Analysis

Glossary of Basic Terms

phonological process: a simplifying tendency on the part of the child to alter natural classes of sounds in a systematic way

phonological process analysis: an attempt to explain a child's substitutions by describing them in terms of general patterns of simplification

6.1 GOAL OF PHONOLOGICAL PROCESS ANALYSIS

The goal of this analysis is to describe a child's syllable initial, final, and ambisyllabic substitutions by a finite set of phonological processes, and to determine the extent to which each process occurs.

6.2 FORMS USED

Lexicon Sheet(s)
3 Consonant Inventory Sheets—Lexical Types (from the Substitution Analysis)
Phonological Processes Sheet
Summary Sheet

6.3 SUMMARY OF STEPS

Summary Box 6.   Steps in Phonological Process Analysis
1. *Determine the phonological processes for the child's substitutions*
2. *Decide to do either a complete or a partial analysis of the child's processes*
3. *Calculate the frequency of each phonological process (recorded on Phonological Process Sheet)*
4. *Summarize most frequent phonological processes*

6.4 DISCUSSION OF PROCEDURES

The attempts to analyze a child's language according to phonological processes have dominated research of both normal and language-delayed children (c.f., review in Ingram, 1976) in recent years. Phonological processes represent descriptions of children's simplifications of adult sounds that group individual changes into general patterns. For example, we can group a child's tendency to drop /s/ in /s/ plus consonant clusters with the tendency to delete /l/ in consonant plus /l/ clusters into a general process of Cluster Reduction. Consequently, such an analysis attempts not just to describe a child's substitutions, but to explain them, although the explanatory power of such analyses will always be only as strong as our understanding of the processes that children use. Table 6 presents a representative list of common phonological processes found in the speech of both normal and language-delayed children, based on Ingram (1980) and Stoel-Gammon (1980).

The steps that follow (Method 1) describe a Phonological Process Analysis that is applied to the Substitution Analysis done in Chapter 5. It is also possible, however, to do a Phonological Process Analysis without having done a Substitution Analysis (Method 2). The method for such an analysis is described in section 6.4.2.

Table 6. Examples of phonological processes as listed on the Phonological Processes Sheet

Syllable Structure Processes

Deletion of Final Consonants (FCD): The deletion of any single consonant that occurs at the end of a syllable.

1. nasals: /-m, -n, -ŋ/ example "come" [kʌ] "cone" [ko] "king" [kɪ]
2. voiced stops: /-b, -d, -g/ example "robe" [ro] "ride" [raɪ] "rug" [rʌ]
3. voiceless stops: /-p, -t, -k/ example "up" [ʌ] "cat" [kæ] "cake" [keɪ]
4. voiced fricatives: /-v, -đ, -z, -ʒ, -dʒ/ example "move" [mu] "teeth" [ti] "rose" [ro] "rouge" [ru] "cage" [keɪ]
5. voiceless fricatives: /-f, -θ, -s, -ʃ, -tʃ/ example "leaf" [li] "tooth" [tu] "ice" [aɪ] "wish" [wɪ] "witch" [wɪ]

Reduction of Consonant Clusters (CR): The deletion of one or more consonants that occur together within the same syllable.

		c/l/-		c/r/-		c/w/-
6.	Liquids:					
	reduced to consonant	"clock" [kak]		"cry" [kaɪ]		"queen" [kin]
	consonant deleted	[lak]		[raɪ]		[win]
	cluster deleted	[ak]		[aɪ]		[in]

		-NC voiced	-NC voiceless
7.	Nasals (N):		
	reduced to consonant	"hand" [hæd]	"stamp" [stæp]
	consonant deleted	[hæn]	[stæm]
	cluster deleted		
	other	[hæ]	[sæ]

		s/C/-
8.	/s/ clusters:	
	reduced to consonant	"stop" [tap]
	consonant deleted	[sap]
	cluster deleted	[ap]

Syllable Deletion and Reduplication:

9. **Reduction of Disyllables (RD):** The deletion of an unstressed syllable that follows a stressed syllable in a two-syllable word. For example, "water" [wa] "paper" [peɪp]
10. **Unstressed Syllable Deletion (USD):** The deletion of an unstressed syllable that precedes a stressed syllable. For example, "banana" [næenə] "potato" [teɪto]
11. **Reduplication (R):** The duplication of a stressed syllable of a word. For example, "water" [wawa] "butter" [bʌbʌ]

Substitution Processes

Fronting: The movement of the tongue from the palatal or velar area to the alveolar area of articulation.

12. of Palatals, i.e., Depalatalization (Dep):

		/ʃ/		/ʒ/
initial	"shoe"	[su]		
intervocalic	"fishing"	[fɪsɪŋ]	"measure"	[mɛzɚ]
final	"fish"	[fɪs]	"rouge"	[ruz]

		/tʃ/		/dʒ/
initial	"chop"	[tsap]	"jump"	[dzʌmp]
intervocalic	"catching"	[kɛtsɪŋ]	"reading"	[ridzɪŋ]
final	"match"	[mæts]	"bridge"	[brɪdz]

13. of Velars (VF):

		/k/		/g/
initial	"key"	[ti]	"go"	[do]
intervocalic	"bucket"	[bʌtɪt]	"beagle"	[bidl̩]
final	"duck"	[dʌt]	"bug"	[bʌd]

Stopping (S): The closure of a narrow opening in the vocal tract in syllable initial position.

14. of Initial Voiceless Fricatives:

/f/	/s/	/θ/	/ʃ/
"foot" [pʊt]	"see" [ti]	"thumb" [tʌm]	"shoe" [ku]

15. of Initial Voiced Fricatives:

/v/	/ð/	/z/
"van" [bæn]	"the" [də]	"zoo" [du]

16. of initial Affricates, i.e., total Stopping:
/tʃ/   /dʒ/
"chop" [tap]   "jump" [dʌmp]

Simplification of Liquids and Nasals

17. Liquid Gliding (LG): The replacement of the liquid sounds initially or intervocalically.
/r/ and /l/ with a glide ([w] or [j])
/r-/ example "race" [weɪs] or [jeɪs]
/l-/ example "lay" [weɪ] or [jeɪ]
/-r-/ example "carry" [kæwi] or [kæji]
/-l-/ example "yellow" [jɛwo] or [jɛjo]
18. Vocalization (V): The replacement of a syllable final liquid /-l/ /-r/ with an oral vowel.
/-r/ example "butter" [bʌto] "pear" [peo]
/-l/ example "table" [teɪbo] "tail" [teɪo]
19. Denasalization (DN): The replacement of a nasal consonant with its oral counterpart, attributable to total closure of the velum.

	initial	intervocalic	final
/m/	"man" [bæn]	"tummy" [tʌbi]	"come" [kʌb]
/n/	"no" [do]	"penny" [pɛdi]	"cone" [kod]
/ŋ/		"singer" [sɪgɚ]	"ring" [rɪg]

Other Substitution Processes

20. Deaffrication (DeA): The change of an affricate into a fricative.
Example   "chop" [ʃap]   "juice" [ʒus]
21. Deletion of Initial Consonants (ICD): The deletion of a consonant in the syllable initial position.
Example   "soup" [up]   "hi" [aɪ]   "we" [i]
22. Apicalization (AP): The shift from a labial to an apical production. For example, "pie" [taɪ]   "bee" [di]   "for" [sor]
23. Labialization (LB): The shift from an articulation with the tongue to one made with the lips. For example, "thumb" [fʌm]

Assimilation Processes

The change of an articulatory feature of a consonant to that of another consonant within the same syllable.
24. Velar Assimilation (VA): The replacement of a nonvelar consonant by a velar one in the environment of a velar consonant. For example, "duck" [gʌk]   "take" [keɪk]
25. Labial Assimilation (LA): The replacement of a nonlabial consonant by a labial one in the environment of a labial consonant. For example, "bed" [dɛd]   "Pete" [tit]
26. Prevocalic Voicing (PV): The change of a voiceless obstruent into a voiced one when preceding a vowel within the same syllable.
For example, "paper" [beɪpɾ]   "table" [deɪbl]   "key" [gi]
27. Devoicing of Final Consonants (FS): The devoicing of a voiced obstruent at the end of a syllable. For example, "dog" [dɔk]   "goes" [gos]

6.4.1   Method 1

Step 1: **Determine the phonological processes for the child's substitutions**

1. Table 7 presents the major substitutions used by children acquiring English, and gives the number of a phonological process in Table 6 that could result in such a substitution.
   a. Start with the initial substitutions circled in red on the Summary Sheet.
   b. For each substitution, see if it occurs on Table 7. If so, look at the phonological process listed in Table 7 and exemplified in Table 6.
   c. Examine the cases of the words in which the substitution occurs on the Consonant Inven-

tory Sheet—Lexical Types (initial sounds) and the complete production on the Lexicon Sheet in order to ascertain if the process accurately describes the change the child has made.
   d. If the process is correct, record this occurrence by finding the process on the Phonological Processes Sheet and circle (in red) the process and the adult sound affected.
   e. If the substitution does not occur in Table 7, leave it until all substitutions accounted for by processes 1 to 27 (on Table 6) are entered. (See h. below.)
   f. If a general process is listed, for example, Fronting of /k-/, look for other substitutes that come under the process before going on to enter an unrelated process.

Table 7. Major substitutions for English consonants and references to potential phonological processes

Sounds			Major Substitutions					Processes

nasals

	[b]	[d]	[n]	∅	[m]
/m/	19		22	1	
/n/		19		1, 7	23
/ŋ/			13	1	

stops

	[b]	[d]	[g]	[p]	[t]	[k]	∅
/p/	26	22, 26			22		3
/b/		22		27			2
/t/		26	24, 26			24	3
/d/			24		27		2, 7
/k/		13, 26	26				3
/g/		13				27	2

Affricates

	[t]	[d]	[ts]	[dz]	∅	[ʃ]	[ʒ]
/tʃ/	12, 16	12, 16 / 26	12		5	20	20, 26
/dʒ/		12		12	4		20

fricatives

	[p]	[t]	[f]	[s]	[ʃ]	∅
/f/	14	14, 22		22		5
/θ/			23	22		5
/s/		14				5, 8 / 21
/ʃ/		12, 14	12			5

	[b]	[d]				∅
/v/	15					4
/ð/		15				4
/z/		15				4
/ʒ/		12, 15				4

Glides

	∅
/w/	21
/j/	21

Liquids

	[w]	∅
/r/	17	6, 21
/l/	17	6, 21

Glottal

	∅
/h/	21

Processes

Deletion of Final Consonants
1. Nasals
2. Voiced stops
3. Voiceless stops
4. Voiced fricatives
5. Voiceless fricatives

Reduction of Consonant Clusters
6. Liquids
7. Nasals
8. /s/ clusters

Syllable deletion and Reduplication
9. Reduction of disyllables
10. Unstressed syllable deletion
11. Reduplication

Fronting
12. of palatals
13. of velars

Stopping
14. of initial voiceless fricatives
15. of initial voiced fricatives
16. of initial affricates

Simplification of Liquids and Nasals
17. Liquid gliding
18. Vocalization
19. Denasalization

Other Substitution Processes
20. Deaffrication
21. Deletion of initial consonants
22. Apicalization
23. Labialization

Assimilation Processes
24. Velar assimilation
25. Labial assimilation
26. Prevocalic voicing
27. Devoicing of final consonants

---

g. Often, two or more processes will affect a substitute at the same time. In these cases, simply enter the substitute separately for each process, for example, [d] for /k-/ in "key" [d] is a substitute that shows both Fronting of Velars (13) and Prevocalic Voicing (26).

h. Continue until all the substitutions have been entered as phonological processes on the Phonological Processes Sheet. Postulate processes for those substitutions not described by processes 1 to 27.

2. Repeat for Ambisyllabic substitutions.
3. Repeat for Final substitutions.
4. Examine data for processes that affect entire syllables (9, 10, 11). Follow these guidelines:

   a. Check for Reduction of Disyllables (9). Examine the Consonant Inventory Sheet—Lexical Types (ambisyllabic) to see if a dash is entered over at least two disyllabic lexical types and indicates the deletion of an unstressed syllable after a stressed one. If so, circle the process on the Phonological Processes Sheet.

   b. Check for Unstressed Syllable Deletion (10). Examine the Lexicon Sheet for cases of adult words with unstressed syllables before stressed ones (e.g., "ba/nana"). If at least two cases show deletion of the unstressed syllable, e.g., "banana" [nænə] or [bænə], circle the process on the Phonological Processes Sheet.

   c. Check for Reduplication (11). Examine the Child Syllable Sheet for cases of reduplication. If at least 2 occur, circle the process on the Phonological Processes Sheet.

Step 2: **Decide to do either a complete or a partial analysis of the child's processes**

If your goal is to get only the most general picture of a child's phonology, you could stop at this point with a summary analysis of the child's processes. This could occur if: 1) the child uses only a small number of processes or 2) there is no immediate need to determine the frequency in which the process occurs. In a summary analysis, skip Step 3 and go right on to Step 4 to summarize the data. Within a partial analysis you can either analyze only the substitutions described by processes 1 to 27 or else all of the child's substitutions. The two measures in Step 4, 1.f. only require an analysis of these substitutions described by the 27 processes in Table 6.

If a more in-depth analysis is desired, decide whether to do a partial or a complete analysis. In a partial analysis, only processes for a child's major substitutions are examined. Notice, for example, that the processes circled in Step 1 are only for patterns of error. So, if a process is not entered, it may be because 1) the child is producing a sound (or sounds) correctly and therefore is not using a process or 2) a lack of data. For example, if Final Consonant Deletion is not circled for voiceless stops, this could either mean that the child produces them correctly, or that the child did not attempt any words with them. A partial analysis does not include this information. Step 3 describes such a partial analysis of the frequency of the phonological processes that account for the child's substitutions. In most cases, such an analysis will be sufficient. When an even more thorough analysis is desired, a complete analysis may be followed.

Step 3: **Calculate the frequency of each phonological process**

Partial Analysis

1. Begin with the first phonological process that is circled on the Phonological Processes Sheet. Locate the instances on the appropriate Consonant Inventory Sheet—Lexical Types. For example, if the first process is Final Consonant Deletion of nasals (1) and only /-n/ is circled, locate lexical types with this segment on the Consonant Inventory Sheet—Lexical Types marked for final segments. If /-m/ or /-ŋ/ are not circled, then do not calculate frequencies for them. This would only be done in a complete analysis.
2. Scan the Lexicon Sheet to find instances where the process has not applied. The numbers of correct productions listed in the far left columns should be helpful in locating these.
3. On the Phonological Processes Sheet, enter the number of lexical types in which the process applies at least once over the number of lexical types in which it could have applied. Do not consider lexical types if the syllable in which the target segment occurs has been deleted. For example, if /-n/ is being examined, "telephone" is not considered if its entry is "telephone" because the child produced [tɛl]. Also do not consider deletions and glottals when calculating proportions for processes such as Fronting and Stopping. For example, if /k-/ shows three [t]'s and three ∅'s, consider Fronting as occurring 1.00 (3/3) rather than three out of six or 0.50.
4. Calculate a proportion for the frequency of occurrence of the process. For example, if the data for /-n/ are as follows: "man" [mæ], "hand" [hæb], "telephone" [tɛl], "can" [kæ], and "own" [op], we get (1) Final Consonant Deletion of nasals, 2/4 or 0.50, and (19) Denasalization, 2/4 or 0.50. A proportion of 0.50 only means that half the items underwent the process involved. It does not mean that the other 0.50 are correct. They may have been affected by another process.

5. To calculate the process (9) Reduction of Disyllables, calculate the proportion of disyllables on the Consonant Inventory Sheet—Lexical Types (ambisyllabic segments) that have been reduced to a monosyllable. To calculate the proportion of Reduplication, calculate the proportion of reduplicated CVCV's, based on the numbers on the Child Syllable Sheet. The formula is:

$$\frac{\text{completely reduplicated CVCV} + \text{partially reduplicated CVCV}}{\text{total number of CVCV phonetic forms}}$$

Complete Analysis

To do a complete analysis, return to the Phonological Processes Sheets and repeat Step 3 for all processes and possible segments affected. This will indicate those cases where processes are infrequent and those where there is a gap in the data.

Step 4: **Summarize most frequent phonological processes**

1. If Step 3 was not done:
   a. List the circled processes from the Phonological Processes Sheets onto the Summary Sheet (bottom).
   b. Place each under its appropriate general category, e.g., Process (18) Vocalization would go under Simplification of Liquids and Nasals.
   c. List on the far left column on the Summary Sheet. Cross out percentages given at the bottom of the Summary Sheet.
   d. Write "Summary analysis" after Phonological Process Analysis on Summary Sheet.
   e. List the segments affected for each process, e.g., if Fronting was only found for initial /k/ and /g/, enter Fronting of Velars /k-/ /g-/. Also enter the number of the process.
   f. Use other columns on Summary Sheet if necessary.
2. If Step 3 was done, enter processes the same way as you did for 1 (above) except for the following differences in steps:
   a. Place each process into the column that reflects its proportion of occurrence, e.g., if Fronting of Velars (VF) is like this on the Phonological Processes Sheets,

Fronting   (13)   of Velars (VF)

syllable position	/k/	/g/	/ŋ/
initial	0.33 (2/6)	0.50 (3/6)	—
intervocalic	—	—	
final	—	0.75 (3/4)	0.67 (2/3)

it would be entered on the Summary Sheet:

FRONTING OF PALATALS AND VELARS		
(13) /k-/	(13) /g-/ /-g/ /-ŋ/	

0.0–0.20	0.21–0.49	0.50–0.79	0.80–.100

b. In a partial analysis, only enter processes and affected segments that meet the Criterion of Frequency as calculated in the Phonetic Analysis. For example, if Fronting of Velars shows /k-/ as 0.33 (2/6), and Fronting of Palatals /ʃ/ 0.50 (4/8), only the latter would be entered on the Summary Sheet if the Criterion of Frequency was 4.

c. The occurrence of affected segments that undergoes a process below the Criterion of Frequency can be entered on the Summary Sheet if the frequency of occurrence combined with another affected segment within the same process meets the criterion, and their proportions of occurrence are the same. For example, if Fronting of Velars shows /-k/ 0.33 (2/6) and /-g/ 0.43 (3/7), and the Criterion of Frequency is 4, then /-k/ /-g/ can be entered on the Summary Sheet because their total occurrence of 4 meets the criterion. The *same* proportion is one that is within one of the four distributions shown on the Summary Sheet, that is, 0–0.20; 0.21–0.49; 0.50–0.79; and 0.80–1.00. Both /-k/ and /-g/ in the above example have proportions within the 0.21–0.49 category.

d. Enter the Number of Processes and Number of Affected Segments onto the Summary Sheet by counting: 1) only the 27 processes given in Table 6, even though others may have been needed to do the analysis, and 2) only those processes and affected segments that occur with a proportion of 0.50 or greater.

6.4.2   Method 2

For those interested in doing a phonological process analysis without a substitution analysis as explained in Chapter 5, the following method is suggested. It is essentially a combination of the procedures in Chapter 5 with those of Chapter 6. Summary Box 7 briefly describes the steps to be discussed.

Summary Box 7.
Steps in Phonological Process Analysis when a Substitution Analysis has not been done

1. *Isolate syllables of adult words*—(same as Step 1 of Substitution Analysis, c.f., Summary Box 5).
2. *Record adult words and sounds attempted*—(same as Step 2 of Substitution Analysis, c.f., Summary Box 5).
3. *Enter child's substitutes, one process at a time*—(following order of processes as listed on the Phonological Processes Sheet).
4. *Calculate the frequency of each phonological process*—(same as Step 3 of Phonological Process Analysis, c.f., Summary Box 6).
5. *Summarize most frequent phonological processes*—(same as Step 4 of Phonological Process Analysis, c.f., Summary Box 6).

Step 1:   **Isolate syllables of adult words**

Step 2:   **Record adult words and sounds attempted**

Any kind of analysis that requires the comparison of adult and child forms has to have a basic organization of the data into syllable initial, final, and ambisyllabic segments. Consequently, the first two steps here are the same as those used in the Substitution Analysis (c.f., section 5.4 for a description of them).

Step 3:   **Enter child's substitutes, one process at a time**

Enter these as described for Step 3 in the Substitution Analysis (Section 5.4) except for the following differences:

1. Enter substitutes by following the phonological processes listed on the Phonological Processes Sheet. For example, the first substitutes entered will be those for the Deletion of Final Consonants.
2. Enter the abbreviation from Table 6 of the process into each box that shows at least two lexical types undergoing the process.
3. After each segment is finished, give a count of the frequency of the process. Use the abbreviations provided on the Phonological Processes Sheet for individual processes. For example, the following display for final /-k/ shows FCD (Final Consonant Deletion) occurring in 3 out of 6 lexical types.

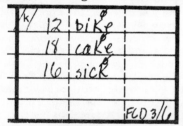

4. The Processes in number 3 on the Phonological Processes Sheet will be skipped at this step because they deal with syllables. Their calculation will occur in Step 4, in concordance with the procedure described in section 6.4.1, Step 4,d.

Step 4:   **Calculate the frequency of each phonological process**

Step 5:   **Summarize most frequent phonological processes**

The last two steps are essentially the same as Steps 3 and 4 in the Phonological Process Analysis (c.f., section 6.4.1 for a discussion of them). Here you will take the processes and their frequencies listed on the Consonant Inventory Sheets and enter them on the Phonological Processes Sheet. The only calculations needed are those for processes that deal with syllables.

6.5   SAMPLE PHONOLOGICAL PROCESS ANALYSIS

6.5.1   Method 1

Sample Analysis 5.5 in Chapter 5 presents the Substitution Analysis for Jennika. These data are used here to exemplify the Steps for Phonological Process Analysis in section 6.4.1. To follow this discussion, refer to Sample Analysis 5.5, Lexicon Sheet 2, and Sample Analyses 5.1, 5.2, and 5.3. All of these sheets are in section 5.5 of Chapter 5.

Step 1 involves identifying the phonological processes for the child's various substitutions. Begin with the initial substitutions on Sample Analysis 5.5. The first substitution circled is [d] for adult /k-/. First, see if this substitute is listed on Table 7. There we find [d] with a reference to processes 13 and 26, which are found on Table 6 to be Fronting of Velars and Voicing, respectively. Next, look at Jennika's Consonant Inventory Sheet (Sample Analysis 5.1) to see the words in which these occur. Those words are "cookie," "kitty," and "Kristen." A check of Lexicon Sheet 2 confirms that the processes are occurring as described in Table 6. Notice also the following points: 1) Jennika's Consonant Inventory Sheet also shows a [g] for /k-/, which is an additional case of Voicing, although not of Fronting, and 2) a glance at the substitutes for /g-/ shows a [d], a case of Fronting, although it occurred only once and therefore was not listed on the Summary Sheet. The Consonant Inventory Sheets can be scanned in this manner to get an idea, from less frequent items, if a process is in effect. We then record the occurrence of Fronting and Voicing by circling these for /k-/ on the Phonological Processes Sheet (c.f., Sample Analysis 6.1).

According to Step 1,1.f, we next look to see if there are other substitutes that show Fronting or Voicing. There are none for the initial substitutes, but there are cases of Fronting for the ambisyllabic and final substitutes. These cases are [t] for /-k-/ and /-k/. These are then circled also on the Phonological Processes Sheet (c.f., Sample Analysis 5.1).

The next substitute for Jennika is ∅ for /s-/. Looking at Table 7, we see that this can be for either process 8, Reduction of Consonant Clusters, or process 21, Deletion of Initial Consonants. When we examine the Consonant Inventory Sheet (Sample Analysis 5.1) to resolve this, we see that the words are "spoon" and "sweater" and that consequently, Consonant Cluster Reduction is involved. This process, then, is circled on the Phonological Processes Sheet.

The last two substitutes for the initial segments are [w] for /r-/ and ∅ for /h-/. A check of Tables 6 and 7 reveals that these represent Gliding and Initial Consonant Deletion, respectively. These are then circled on the Phonological Processes Sheet at the appropriate places.

Because we have already entered the one instance of an ambisyllabic substitute, we can now turn to the final substitutes. A first glance reveals

that a number of (∅) deletions are entered, which indicates widespread Final Consonant Deletion for some of the stops, and for the voiceless fricative /-s/. These are entered on the Phonological Processes Sheet. Next, there is a [t] for /θ/, an isolated case of Stopping. Note, however, that process 14 on Table 6 is restricted to initial voiceless fricatives. Therefore, this substitution cannot be described by the process on Table 6. Later, it can be described as a case of Final Stopping and can be entered as an unnumbered process. The deletion of /-r/ is also not accounted for by Table 6 because FCD does not include liquids. It, too, will be entered as an unnumbered process of Final Deletion of Liquids. The last substitute to be explained is [m] for /-n/. When we examine Table 7, we find this substitute entered as process 23. Turning to the Consonant Inventory Sheet for final segments (Sample Analysis 5.3), we find the words "down," "spoon," "alldone," and "getdown," which are [dʌm] [pʌm] [ædʌm] and [didʌm] on Lexicon Sheet 2. It seems that Jennika has a straightforward substitution of [m] for /-n/. We now turn to Step 1,4., which involves syllable processes. For process 9, Reduction of Disyllables, we examine Sample Analysis 5.2 to see if disyllables are reduced. This can be found—[wa] for "rosy" and [waʃ] for "sweater"—so the process is circled. Lexicon Sheet 2 shows no words having initial unstressed syllables so Unstressed Syllable Deletion cannot be determined. Last, we can see from Sample Analysis 3.6, which is Jennika's Child Syllable Sheet, that 15 instances of reduplication occur, so this process also is entered.

In Step 2, we need to decide whether to do a complete analysis. Because Jennika has only a small number of processes, we could decide to do just a partial analysis. Here, a summary analysis and partial analysis will be demonstrated.

In a summary analysis, you skip Step 3 and go on in Step 4,1. to list the processes circled on the Phonological Processes Sheet. This sheet for Jennika shows that the first process with circled items is the Deletion of Final Consonants, specifically the voiceless stops /-t, -k/ and the voiceless fricative /-s/. These are listed in the far right column of the Summary Sheet. Sample Analysis 6.2 shows a Summary Sheet for Jennika with the phonological processes listed according to Step 4,1.

For a *partial analysis*, we go to Step 3,1. and calculate the proportion of times processes occur. Beginning with Final Consonant Deletion, we can turn to the Consonant Inventory Sheet for final consonants (Sample Analysis 5.3) to see how often it occurs. For process 2, we have two cases of a deleted /d/ so we enter 1.00 (2/2). For /-t/ we get two cases of a final consonant, "hat" and "hot," and three cases of deletion, "out," "blanket," and "get" for 0.60 (3/5). Last, /-k/ shows deletion in three out of seven cases for 0.43. For /-s/ we get two deletions in five cases, with two phonetic types showing substitutions ([ʃ] and [t]), and one with a correct [s] ("juice"). Here, notice that the inclusion of "icecream" is problematic because the form [dʒudʒu] could be described as Reduplication of the second syllable. In this case, however, there is no serious difficulty because the proportions of deletion with or without it included, 0.40 versus 0.25, both fall into the same frequency range on the Summary Sheet.

For the Cluster Reduction of /s-/, we refer to the Consonant Inventory Sheet for initial segments (Sample Analysis 5.1). There we find that deletion took place in both words with /s/ clusters. To calculate the frequency of process 9, the Reduction of Disyllables, we look at Sample Analysis 5.2, which shows the child's disyllables. There are 13 disyllables in all, counting correct productions, for example, entry 13 for "daddy" and those with substitutes, for example, "Kristen." Notice that "Kristen" and "blanket" are entered twice because they have medial clusters and, therefore, need to be counted once each. Also, "cookie" has three different phonetic types, so it is counted three times. There are two deleted disyllables, "sweater" and "rosy," so our proportion is 0.15 (2/13). As explained in Step 3,5., Reduplication is determined from the Child Syllable Sheet for CVCV syllables. Jennika's Child Syllable Sheet, which is Sample Analysis 3.1, shows 15 reduplications out of 19, for a rate of 0.79 (15/19).

For Fronting of /k/, we find that this occurred three out of five times in the initial position, with one phonetic type, "cookie," showing an unfronted [g]. The [dʒ] in "icecream" is not considered a case of Fronting because the target has not moved to the alveolar position. The same proportion occurs for intervocalic /-k-/. For final /-k-/, it occurs in two of three cases. The count must be taken carefully because there are three cases of deletion and one glottal stop. Fronting, however, only refers to a tendency that results when the tongue is used in the production of /k/. If the tongue is not used, it does not mean that Fronting does not apply, but rather that the distinction is not relevant. These proportions, as well as those for the other processes found in Jennika, are provided in Sample Analysis 6.1.

The last step is to place the processes and the segments affected onto the Summary Sheet. Unlike the summary analysis, here we place them into separate columns depending on their proportion of occurrences. Sample Analysis 6.3 shows this placement.

6.5.2 Method 2

To demonstrate Method 2 with the data on Jennika, we can go to Step 3, which involves entering the child's substitutes on the Consonant Inventory Sheets. After Step 3, Jennika would have three Consonant Inventory Sheets like Sample Analyses 5.1, 5.2, and 5.3, but the substitutes would not be entered. We would begin to enter the substitutes by taking the first process on the Phonological Processes Sheet, the Deletion of Final Consonants, as stated in Step 3,1. (section 6.4.2). We would then turn to the Consonant Inventory Sheet with final segments (Sample Analysis 5.3) and enter the substitutes and deletions that occur. After that step has been completed, this sheet will look the same as Sample Analysis 5.3. Step 3,2. states that we identify those segments with at least two lexical types undergoing a process. Those segments that need to be so marked are /-d/, /-t/, /-k/, and /s/. Here is how the boxes for /-d/ and /-t/ would look on the Consonant Inventory Sheet.

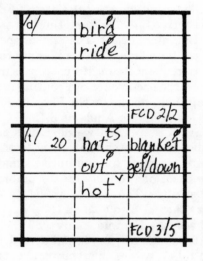

For /-d/, FCD 2/2 means that Final Cosonant Deletion occurs twice in both lexical types with a syllable final /-d/. For /-t/, FCD 3/5 means that the process occurred in three of the five possible places. Do the counts for /-k/, /-s/, and /-r/ on Sample Analysis 5.3. They should be FCD 3/7, 2/5, and 2/2, respectively.

The next process is Reduction of Consonant Clusters. For the liquid and /s/ clusters, these would be entered on the Consonant Inventory Sheet for initial segments (Sample Analysis 5.1). The only clusters in which at least two lexical types occur showing the process are the /s/C–ones, with "spoon" and "sweater" both showing deletion. In the /s–/ box, we would enter CR 2/2. We process in this fashion until all the substitutes have been entered.

For Step 4, we simply transfer the information about the occurrence of processes from the Consonant Inventory Sheets onto the Phonological Processes Sheet (c.f., Step 3 of Method 1). After Step 4, this sheet will look as it does in Sample Analysis 6.1. Step 5 is done in the same way as Step 4 of Method 1, in which the processes are summarized on the Summary Sheet. After this step, the Summary Sheet will look as it does in Sample Analysis 6.2.

6.6 Practice Data

Practice Page 6.1 is a Summary Sheet that summarizes the Substitution Analysis of the data for R, from Lexicon Sheet 3 (c.f., Appendix E). Practice Method 1 by entering the phonological processes used by R onto Practice Page 6.2, which is a blank Phonological Processes Sheet. Do this by following the steps outlined in Summary Box 6 and described in 6.4.1. Use Tables 6 and 7 to determine the processes that occur. Lexicon Sheet 3 for R is also included here to facilitate the checking of the phonetic types for individual lexical types. Appendix F contains the results of this analysis, which can be used for comparison when you are finished, a completed Summary Sheet (F.1), and a Phonological Processes Sheet (F.2).

After doing Method 1, attempt Method 2 (Summary Box 7). Practice Pages 6.3, 6.4, and 6.5 which are Consonant Inventory Sheets with R's lexical types listed *before* substitutions have been entered, are provided to help you with Method 2. Enter the substitutions (in red) on a process by process basis and compare your results with the Consonant Inventory Sheets in Appendix E (E.3, E.4, and E.5). Next, calculate the processes and compare the results with those on the completed Phonological Processes Sheet from Method 1 (F.3). They should be the same.

PHONOLOGICAL PROCESSES SHEET

Child's name and age _Jennika 1;5_

Syllable Structure Processes

Deletion of Final Consonants (FCD):

(1) nasals: /-m/ /-n/ /-ŋ/
_____ _____

(3) voiceless stops: /-p/ /-t/ /-k/
_____ (0.60 (3/5)) (0.43 (3/7))

(2) voiced stops: /-b/ /-d/ /-g/
_____ (1.00 (3/2)) _____

(4) voiced fricatives: /-v/ /-ð/ /-z/ /-dʒ/
_____ _____ _____ _____

(5) voiceless fricatives: /-f/ /-θ/ /-s/ /-ʃ/ /-tʃ/
_____ _____ (0.40 (2/5)) _____ _____

Liquids /-r/
(1.00 (2/2))

Reduction of Consonant Clusters (CR):

	(6) Liquids		(7) Nasals		(8) /s/ clusters
	C/l/-	C/r/-	-NCvd	-NCvless	/s/C-
reduced to C	_____	_____	_____	_____	(1.00 (3/2))
C deleted	_____	_____	_____	_____	_____
cluster deleted	_____	_____	_____	_____	
Total	_____	_____	_____	_____	(1.00 (3/2))

Syllable Deletion

(9) Reduction of Disyllables (RD) (0.15 (2/13))

(10) Unstressed syllable deletionUSD) _____

(11) Reduplication (0.79 (15/19))

Substitution Processes

Fronting

(12) of Palatals (PF)

syllable position	/ʃ/	/ʒ/	/tʃ/	/dʒ/
initial	_____	_____	_____	_____
intervocalic	_____	_____	_____	_____
final	_____	_____	_____	_____

(13) of Velars (VF)

	/k/	/g/	/ŋ/
initial	(0.60 (3/5))	_____	_____
intervocalic	(0.60 (3/5))	_____	_____
final	(0.60 (2/3))	_____	_____

Stopping (S)

(14) of Initial Voiceless Fricatives

/f/	/θ/	/s/	/ʃ/
_____	_____	_____	_____

(15) of Initial Voiced Fricatives

/v/	/ð/	/z/	/ʒ/
_____	_____	_____	_____

(16) of Affricates

/tʃ/	/dʒ/
_____	_____

Simplification of Liquids and Nasals

(17) Liquid Gliding (LG))

substitutes   substitutes

/r-/ [w] ⟨1.00 (3/3)⟩   [j] _____   /-r-/ [w] _____   [j] _____

/l-/ [w] _____   [j] _____   /-l-/ [w] _____   [j] _____

(18) Vocalization (V):

/ɹ/ [ ] _____   [ ] _____   [ ] _____   [ ] _____

/l̩/ [ ] _____   [ ] _____   [ ] _____   [ ] _____

(19) Denasalization (DN):

	initial	intervocalic	final	total
/m/	_____	_____	_____	_____
/n/	_____	_____	_____	_____
/ŋ/		_____	_____	_____

Other Substitution Processes

Process	Target	Change	Syllable position	
(21) Deletion of	/ /	[ ]	_____	_____
Initial Consonants	/ h /	[∅]	initial	⟨1.00 (3/3)⟩
(23) Labialization	/ n /	[m]	final	⟨.75 (3/4)⟩
	/ /	[ ]	_____	_____
Finial Stopping	/ θ /	[+]	final	⟨1.00 (2/2)⟩
	/ /	[ ]	_____	_____
	/ /	[ ]	_____	_____
	/ /	[ ]	_____	_____

Assimilation Processes

Process	Sounds	Change	Environment	
(26) Prevocalic	/ /	[ ]	_____	_____
voicing	/ k /	[d]	initial	⟨1.00 (5/5)⟩
	/ /	[ ]	_____	_____
	/ /	[ ]	_____	_____
	/ /	[ ]	_____	_____
	/ /	[ ]	_____	_____
	/ /	[ ]	_____	_____
	/ /	[ ]	_____	_____

SUMMARY SHEET

Child's name and age _Jennika 1,5_

Sample **lexical**   **phonetic**   **phonetic**   **phonetic**
size **types:** _____ **types:** _____ **tokens:** _____ **forms:** _____

Phonetic Analysis   Articulation Score _____

Total Number of Sounds _____   Criterion of Frequency _____   ($\overline{2} = \overline{25}$)
word initial _____   word medial _____   word final _____

syllable   **most**   **Proportion**   **Closed**
types: **frequent:** _____ **of:** _____ Monosyllables _____ **syllables**

Analysis of Homonymy
Ratio of Homonymous forms _____:1   Homonymous types _____:1
Proportion of Homonymous forms _____   Homonymous types _____

Substitution Analysis

	m	n	ŋ	p	b	t	d	k	g	tʃ	dʒ	f	θ	s	ʃ	v	ð	z	ʒ	w	j	r	l	h	
I			▓																▓						___
A																									___
F																			▓	▓				▓	___

Proportion of Data _____ (/67) and Matches _____ (/) Acquired sounds _____

Phonological Process Analysis   Number of: _____ Processes _____ Affected Segments

Summary Analysis   FINAL CONSONANT DELETION

(2)/-d/ (3) /-t,-k/		
(5) /-s / Liquid Deletion /-r/		

REDUCTION OF CONSONANT CLUSTERS

(8) /s/c -		

SYLLABLE DELETION AND REDUPLICATION

(9) Reduction of Disyllables		
(11) Reduplication		

FRONTING OF PALATALS AND VELARS

(13)/k-, -k-, -k/		

STOPPING OF FRICATIVES AND AFFRICATES

Final Stopping /-θ/		

SIMPLIFICATION OF LIQUIDS AND NASALS

(17) Gliding /r-/		

OTHER PROCESSES

(21) Deletion of Initial Consonants /h-/		
(23) Labialization /-n/		
(26) Voicing /k-/		

SUMMARY SHEET

Child's name and age _Jennika 1;5_

| Sample size | lexical types: _____ | phonetic types: _____ | phonetic tokens: _____ | phonetic forms: _____ |

Phonetic Analysis   Articulation Score _____
Total Number of Sounds _____   Criterion of Frequency _____ ($\overline{2} = \overline{25}$)
word initial _____   word medial _____   word final _____

| syllable types: | most frequent: _____ | Proportion of: _____ | Monosyllables _____ | Closed syllables |

Analysis of Homonymy
Ratio of Homonymous forms _____:1   Homonymous types _____:1
Proportion of Homonymous forms _____   Homonymous types _____

Substitution Analysis

	m	n	ŋ	p	b	t	d	k	g	tʃ	dʒ	f	θ	s	ʃ	v	ð	z	ʒ	w	j	r	l	h	
I			▨																▨						___
A																									___
F																				▨	▨			▨	___

Proportion of Data _____ (/67) and Matches _____ (/) Acquired sounds _____

Phonological Process Analysis   Number of: __9__ Processes __10__ Affected Segments

Partial Analysis   FINAL CONSONANT DELETION

| | (3) /-k/ | (3) /-t/ | (2) /-d/ |
| | (5) /-s/ | | Deletion /-r/ |

REDUCTION OF CONSONANT CLUSTERS

| | | | (8) /s/c - |
| | | | |

SYLLABLE DELETION AND REDUPLICATION

| (9) Red. of Disyllables | | (11) Reduplication | |
| | | | |

FRONTING OF PALATALS AND VELARS

| | | (13) /k-,-k-,-k / | |
| | | | |

STOPPING OF FRICATIVES AND AFFRICATES

| | | | Stopping /-θ/ |
| | | | |

SIMPLIFICATION OF LIQUIDS AND NASALS

| | | | (17) /r-/ |
| | | | |

OTHER PROCESSES

		(23) Labialization /-n/	(21) Deletion /h-/
			(26) Voicing /k-/

| 0.0–0.20 | 0.21–0.49 | 0.50–0.79 | 0.80–.100 |

SUMMARY SHEET

Child's name and age __R___ _3;11_____

| Sample size | lexical types: _____ | phonetic types: _____ | phonetic tokens: _____ | phonetic forms: _____ |

Phonetic Analysis   Articulation Score _____

Total Number of Sounds _____ Criterion of Frequency _____ ($\overline{2} = \overline{25}$)

word initial _____ word medial _____ word final _____

| syllable types: | most frequent: _____ | Proportion of: _____ | Monosyllables _____ | Closed syllables |

Analysis of Homonymy

Ratio of Homonymous forms _____:1   Homonymous types _____:1

Proportion of Homonymous forms _____   Homonymous types _____

Substitution Analysis

	m	n	ŋ	p	b	t	d	k	g	tʃ	dʒ	f	θ	s	ʃ	v	ð	z	ʒ	w	j	r	l	h	
I	ⓝ		▨	✓	(f p)	(d g s)	ⓓ		–		(p h)	–	∅		–	–	–		▨	(p d)	–	(w t)	ⓗ	
A	ⓝ	∅		–		(d ∅)	✓	ⓖ		–		–	–	✓	–		–	–		–	∅	–	
F	✓	∅		(t)	(p)	(p ∅ t)	✓	–	–		–	(f)	✓	–		–	▨			∅ ∅	

Proportion of Data _____ (/67) and Matches _____ (/) Acquired sounds _____

Phonological Process Analysis   Number of: _____ Processes _____ Affected Segments

FINAL CONSONANT DELETION

REDUCTION OF CONSONANT CLUSTERS

SYLLABLE DELETION AND REDUPLICATION

FRONTING OF PALATALS AND VELARS

STOPPING OF FRICATIVES AND AFFRICATES

SIMPLIFICATION OF LIQUIDS AND NASALS

OTHER PROCESSES

| 0.0–0.20 | 0.21–0.49 | 0.50–0.79 | 0.80–.100 |

PHONOLOGICAL PROCESSES SHEET

Child's name and age ___R___ 3;11 _____

Syllable Structure Processes

Deletion of Final Consonants (FCD):

(1) nasals: /-m/ /-n/ /-ŋ/
_____ _____ _____

(3) voiceless stops: /-p/ /-t/ /-k/
_____ _____ _____

(2) voiced stops: /-b/ /-d/ /-g/
_____ _____ _____

(4) voiced fricatives: /-v/ /-ð/ /-ʒ/ /-dʒ/
_____ _____ _____ _____

(5) voiceless fricatives: /-f/ /-θ/ /-s/ /-ʃ/ /-tʃ/
_____ _____ _____ _____ _____

Reduction of Consonant Clusters (CR):

	(6) Liquids		(7) Nasals		(8) /s/ clusters
	C/l/-	C/r/-	-NCvd	-NCvless	/s/C-
reduced to C	_____	_____	_____	_____	_____
C deleted	_____	_____	_____	_____	_____
cluster deleted	_____	_____	_____	_____	_____
Total	_____	_____	_____	_____	_____

Syllable Deletion

(9) Reduction of Disyllables (RD) _____

(10) Unstressed syllable deletion USD) _____

(11) Reduplication _____

Substitution Processes

Fronting

(12) of Palatals (PF)

syllable position	/ʃ/	/ʒ/	/tʃ/	/dʒ/
initial	_____	_____	_____	_____
intervocalic	_____	_____	_____	_____
final	_____	_____	_____	_____

(13) of Velars (VF)

	/k/	/g/	/ŋ/
	_____	_____	_____
	_____	_____	_____
	_____	_____	_____

Stopping (S)

(14) of Initial Voiceless Fricatives

/f/	/θ/	/s/	/ʃ/
_____	_____	_____	_____

(15) of Initial Voiced Fricatives

/v/	/ð/	/z/	/ʒ/
_____	_____	_____	_____

(16) of Affricates

/tʃ/	/dʒ/
_____	_____

Simplification of Liquids and Nasals

(17) Liquid Gliding (LG))

	substitutes				substitutes		
/r-/	[w] _____	[j] _____		/-r-/	[w] _____	[j] _____
/l-/	[w] _____	[j] _____		/-l-/	[w] _____	[j] _____

(18) Vocalization (V):

/r/	[ ] _____	[ ] _____	[ ] _____	[ ] _____
/l/	[ ] _____	[ ] _____	[ ] _____	[ ] _____

(19) Denasalization (DN):

	initial	intervocalic	final	total
/m/	_____	_____	_____	_____
/n/	_____	_____	_____	_____
/ŋ/		_____	_____	_____

Other Substitution Processes

Process	Target	Change	Syllable position	
_____	/ /	[ ]	_____	_____
_____	/ /	[ ]	_____	_____
_____	/ /	[ ]	_____	_____
_____	/ /	[ ]	_____	_____
_____	/ /	[ ]	_____	_____
_____	/ /	[ ]	_____	_____
_____	/ /	[ ]	_____	_____
_____	/ /	[ ]	_____	_____

Assimilation Processes

Process	Sounds	Change	Environment	
_____	/ /	[ ]	_____	_____
_____	/ /	[ ]	_____	_____
_____	/ /	[ ]	_____	_____
_____	/ /	[ ]	_____	_____
_____	/ /	[ ]	_____	_____
_____	/ /	[ ]	_____	_____
_____	/ /	[ ]	_____	_____
_____	/ /	[ ]	_____	_____

Child's name and age ___R 3;11___

types		types		types		types	
lexical	phonetic	lexical	phonetic	lexical	phonetic	lexical	phonetic
1. apple	hæpo	29. duck	gʌk	55. moon	mu	83. waffle	pafo
2. arm	nan	30. elephant	tʌtʌt	56. one	wʌn	84. water	dʌdo
3. baby	bebi	31. feet	pat	57. paper	peto	85. web	wɛp
	bebe	32. fire	ha	58. pear	peo	86. whale	weo
4. ball	po	33. fireman	hanan	59. pie	paɪ	87. wheel	heo
5. banana	nænʌ	34. fish	pʌsə	60. robe	wop	88. whistle	pɛsɪf
6. basket	sʌkə(2x)	35. flower	ha	61. rock	wak	89. window	dʌdo
7. bathtub	bʌfʌt	36. foot	pat	62. safe	fef	90. witch	wɪtʃ
8. bear	peo	37. fork	pak	63. seagull	sigo		
9. bed	tʌt	38. hammer	næno	64. seed	si		
10. bee	bi	39. hand	nan	65. shoe	suwə		
11. belt	tap	40. hat	hat(2x)		sup		
12. bird	bo	41. high	haɪ	66. shovel	tʌbo		
13. boat	tap	42. horsie	hɔrsi	67. slide	taɪ		
14. book	bʌk		sɔrsi	68. snake	sek		
15. boy	pɔɪ		sʌsi	69. spider	dʌdo		
16. broom	num	43. house	haʊs	70. star	da		
17. brush	bʌʃ	44. king	kin	71. stick	sʌk		
18. butter	dʌdo		kɪn	72. stove	dov		
19. candy	dægi	45. kitty cat	kitat	73. table	tebo		
20. comb	kom	46. ladder	dado	74. tail	tejo		
21. cow	daʊ	47. letter	tato	75. tea	ti		
22. cup	pat	48. light	taɪt	76. teeth	tʌf		
23. desk	sʌk		daɪt	77. telephone	tʌpo		
24. doctor	gaga	49. man	næn	78. tent	tat		
25. dog	kʼak(2x)		nan	79. too	to		
	dɔk	50. marble	babo	80. top	tat		
	gak	51. meat	mit		pat		
26. door	do	52. milk	naʊk	81. towel	taʊ		
27. dress	sæs	53. mommy	mami(2x)		tajo		
28. drum	lam	54. momma	mama	82. tractor	gagɔ		

CONSONANT INVENTORY SHEET
Lexical Types   Child's name and age R 3;11

✓ initial   _____ ambisyllabic   _____ final

b 3	ᵖball ‾banana	d 25	ˢdesk ᵍdoctor	dʒ		g 63		
7	ᵖbear ˢbasket	26	ᵏdog					
10	ᵗbed ᵖboy		ˢdress					
12	ᵗbelt ⁿbroom		ˡdrum					
14,17	ᵗboat ᵈbutter		ᵍduck					
p 57	ᵈspider	t 73	ᵈstove ᵍtractor	tʃ		k 20	ᵈcow ᵈcandy	
58		74	ᵈstar ᵖbath/tub			44	ᵖcup ᵗkitty/cat	
59		75	ᵒstick			45		
		76	ᵖtop					
		⑦⑦						
v		z		ʒ		ð		
f	ᵖfeet	s 63	ᶠsafe ᵒspider	ʃ	ˢshoe ᵗshovel	θ		
	ʰfire	64	ᵗslide					
	ᵖfish ᵐflower	68	ᵒstar					
	ᵖfoot tele/phone	71	ᵒstove					
	ᵖfork							
w 56	ʰwheel ᵖwaffle	l	ᵗᵈlight ᵈladder	r	ᵒbroom ᵒtractor	h 40	ⁿhand ⁿhammer	
85	ᵈwater		ᵒslide ᵗletter		ᵒbrush ʷrock	41	ˢhorsie	
86	ᵖwhistle				ᵒdress	42		
90	ᵈwindow				ᵒdrum	43		
					ʷrobe			
						vowel	ʰarm ʰapple	ᵗelephant
m 51	ⁿman	n 5	ᵖshake			ŋ		
53	ⁿmilk ᵇmarble							
54								
55								

Practice Page 6.4   CONSONANT INVENTORY SHEET

Lexical Types   Child's name and age R   3;11

____ initial   ✓ ambisyllabic   ____ final

b			d		dʒ			g	
3			46	candy					
50			69						
73			89						

p		paper	t	butter / doctor / tractor / water / kittycat	tʃ			k 6	doctor / tractor
1									

v		shovel	z		ʒ			ð	

f		elephant	s	basket	ʃ			θ	
83			42						
			88						

w		flower	l	elephant / telephone	r 42		horsie / marble	h	

								vowel	

m		hammer / fireman	n	candy / window				ŋ	
53			5						
54									

CONSONANT INVENTORY SHEET
Lexical Types Child's name and age R 3;11

____ initial   ____ ambisyllabic   ✓ final

b	robe^p bathtub^t		d	bed^t		dʒ			g	dog^k	
	web^b			bird^ø							
				hand^ø							
				seed^t							
				slide^ø							
p	cup^t		**t** 30	belt^p	basket^ø	**tʃ** 90			**k** 14		
	top^t		31	boat^t					23		
			36						29		
			40						37		
			(45)						(52)		
v 72			**z**			**ʒ**			**ð**		
f 62			**s** 27	desk^ø		**ʃ** 17	fish^v		**θ**		bath^f tub
			43								teeth^f
w			**l**	ball^ø	apple^o	**r**	arm^ø	ladder^o	**h**		
				belt^f	marble^o		bear^ø	butter^o			
				tail^o	shovel^o		door^ø	doctor^∧			
				whale^ø	table^o		fire^ø	hammer^o			
				wheel	waffle^ø		pear^ø	flower^-			
				towel^ø,o	whistle^f		star	letter^o	vowel	shoe^p	
				seagull				paper^o			
								spider^o			
								tractor^o			
								water^o			
m 16	arm^n		**n** 33	moon^ø	elephant^ø				**ŋ** 44	king^n	
20			39	tent^t	telephone^ø						
28			49								
			56								

CHAPTER 7

Some Preliminary Norms of Phonological Development

7.1 A STUDY OF PHONOLOGICAL DEVELOPMENT IN NORMAL AND LANGUAGE-DELAYED CHILDREN

The explicit procedures for phonological analysis that are presented in Chapters 2 through 6 were developed in a way that should allow standardized results to be produced as data accumulate from a variety of children. Some general results from a preliminary investigation (Ingram, 1980) in which these procedures have been applied to the analysis of phonological data from 15 normal and 15 language-delayed children are provided here as, at least, an initial basis of comparison. These results are not intended to resolve the question of difference between the two groups, but they can be used to get a general picture of the ability of any particular child the reader may analyze through these procedures. (For details, see Ingram, 1980.)

The 15 normal children were between the ages of 1;5 and 2;2. The data on these children provide a sample of phonological development during the active period of development from around the 50th word and after (c.f., Ingram, 1976). The data comprise that of children observed by the author, as well as information found in published works (c.f., Table 8).

The data from the 15 language-delayed children also has been accumulated from a variety of

sources—published works, data collected by the author, and unpublished data supplied to the author by practicing language clinicians (c.f., Table 9). A range of data was selected for both populations to ensure a wide sampling of children and to enable us to determine potential speech patterns. All transcriptions were standardized by the procedures described in Section 2.4.3, and all data were placed on Lexicon Sheets as described in that section.

7.1.1 Results of the phonetic analysis

First, we can look at the two gross measures of phonetic ability presented in Chapter 2—Total Number of Sounds and Articulation Scores—to see the range of phonetic ability and the way the two groups compare. Table 10 lists these figures for the 30 subjects.

The mean articulation score for the two groups is the same, 38, indicating that they are reasonably well matched in terms of the number of sounds they can produce. This matching suggests that children who come under study as phonologically delayed between the ages of 4;0 and 8;0 are at a functional level that is equivalent to that of a normal child between 1;6 and 2;0. The median Articulation Score is 40, and it can be used as a relative score for dividing children into groups of low or high performers. This point will again be mentioned in section 7.6 where we will attempt to develop a profile for the comparison of children to these results.

Table 8. Names, sources, ages, and sample sizes of the 15 normal children studied

Child	Age	Sample size lexical types	Sample size phonetic types	Investigator
Hildegard	1;5	30	35	Leopold (1947)
Jennika	1;5	42	73	father's diary
Molly	1;6	47	53	Holmes (1927)
Philip	1;7	82	90	Adams (1972)
Jacob	1;8	81	128	Menn (1976)
Jon	1;8	53	68	unpublished data
Amy	1;8–1;9	50	75	unpublished data
M (girl)	1;9	66	68	Foulke and Stinchfield (1929)
R (boy)	1;10	275	317	Foulke and Stinchfield (1929)
Daniel	1;10–2;0	55	61	Menn (1971)
Joan	1;11	175	185	Velten (1943)
Jennifer	1;11	112	138	unpublished data
Ruth	2;0	333	368	Hills (1914)
DeCamp (boy)	2;1	69	73	DeCamp (1946)
A	2;2	233	233	Smith (1973)

The scores for the Total Number of Sounds are also similar for the two groups of children. They range from a total of 7 to as many as 20 sounds acquired. The average and median Total Number of Sounds Acquired is 14. Regarding word position, the groups are also the same. Both have a mean of 8 initial sounds acquired, with final and medial positions showing on half as many sounds. Performance on final segments is slightly better than on medial ones.

Next, we can look at the actual segments produced by the 30 subjects for each of the three word positions. Table 11 presents information on the number of subjects who used a sound transition to criterion, or to at least twice criterion (c.f., discussion in Chapter 3, section 3.4, Step 5). Table 11 only shows sounds used by at least one-third (i.e., 10) of all subjects. If we set a criterion that at least 50% (15) of

the subjects must use a sound in order for it to be considered "characteristic" or "acquired," and if other less used sounds are transitional, we can then propose the following inventories of sounds (parentheses indicate transitional sounds):

Initial			Medial			Final		
(m)	n		(m)			(m)	n	
b	d	(g)	b	d		p	t	k
p	t	k	(p)	(t)				
(f)	(s)	h						
w								

In Ingram (1976), the following phonetic inventory (for initial sounds only) was proposed as a basic easy set of consonants, as determined from data from four normal children.

Table 9. Names, sources, ages, and sample sizes of the 15 language-delayed children studied

Child	Age	Sample size lexical types	Sample size phonetic types	Investigator
J	3;11	131	131	Weiner (1979)
Kris	3;11	85	103	unpublished data
Ron	3;11	90	101	unpublished data
Billy	4;1	136	159	unpublished data
#9 (girl)	4;10	73	73	Jordan (1976)
Adam	5;0	60	62	unpublished data
#6 (boy)	5;2	72	72	Jordan (1976)
Kevin	5;4	109	129	unpublished data
Ricky	5;11	162	172	unpublished data
John	5;11	93	93	Shriberg & Kwiatkowski (1980)
Ethel I	6;0	65	76	Hinckley (1915)
Bill	6;0	139	139	unpublished data
Darren	6;3	120	137	Grunwell (1977)
Rosie	6;4	47	48	Grunwell (1975)
Tanya	8;0	121	151	Grunwell (1977)

Table 10. The Total Number of Sounds Produced for three word positions, and the Articulation Scores (AS) for 15 normal and 15 language-delayed children

| Child | Normal children Sounds Acquired | | | | | Child | Language-delayed children Sounds Acquired | | | | |
	Initial	Medial	Final	Total	AS		Initial	Medial	Final	Total	AS
Hildegard	3	4	0	7	18	#9 (girl)	5(2)	0(1)	2(3)	7(6)	23
DeCamp	9(4)	0(1)	2	11(5)	28	Ethel I	6	2(3)	0	8(3)	24
Jennika	5	4	3	12	31	J	9(4)	2(3)	1(1)	9(4)	28
Amy	6(2)	3	4	13(2)	31	Kevin	5(2)	2	3(3)	10(5)	29
Molly	7	3	3	13	32	Kris	6(3)	3(2)	2	11(5)	32
Jacob	8(3)	0(3)	4(3)	12(9)	36	Rosie	8	6	0	14	35
Philip	8(1)	6(1)	0	14(2)	39	Adam	11	3	1	15	37
Daniel	5	0	10	15	40	Billy	7(1)	1(5)	3(5)	11(11)	40
M (girl)	10(1)	2(1)	6	18(3)	41	#6 (boy)	10(5)	1(4)	3(1)	14(10)	41
Ruth	8	2(4)	5(4)	15(8)	43	John	6(3)	3(4)	4(2)	13(9)	43
A (boy)	5(2)	5(2)	4(2)	14(6)	44	Tanya	12	1(3)	5	18	43
R (boy)	9(4)	0(4)	7(5)	16(13)	45	Ricky	9(6)	0	6(4)	15(10)	45
Jon	11	3	5	19	47	Darren	8(1)	2(3)	3(4)	13(8)	46
Joan	8	2(3)	7(3)	17(6)	48	Bill	9(1)	3(4)	5	17(5)	46
Jennifer	11(1)	4(3)	5	20(4)	49	Ron	11	3(6)	4(3)	18(9)	52
Mean	8(1)	3(2)	4(1)	14(4)	38	Mean	8(2)	2(3)	3(2)	13(6)	38

```
m   n
b   d
p   t
f   s   h
w       j
```

The above data show no evidence of general use of [j], and they show the later acquisition of [f] [s] as well as the earlier use of [k] and [g]. The inventories suggested above are a representative inventory of sounds that can be used for comparative purposes to determine an individual child's stage of acquisition in producing initial, medial, and final sounds.

The last aspect to present for the Phonetic Analysis is that of syllable structure. It is well known that the earliest syllables for young children are CV and CVC (c.f., Ingram, 1979) but we need to know more about the patterns across children in using them. The two measures of syllable structure discussed in Chapter 2 were devised for this purpose. The first, the Proportion of Monosyllables, deals with the fact that children's preferences for monosyllables over multisyllabic productions vary greatly. The second measure, the Proportion of Closed Syllables, examines the extent to which a child used closed (or CVC) syllable types. Table 12 presents the data on both these measures for the 15 normal and 15 delayed subjects.

The data for the two groups are presented separately because they show differences of which you should be aware (c.f., Ingram, 1980 for detailed anal-

ysis). Regarding the Proportion of Monosyllables, normal children show three levels on this measure: I—high use of monosyllables (0.80–1.00); II—moderate (0.60–0.79); and III—low (0.59 and below). The delayed children show a more limited range on this measure (0.52–0.79), and none of these children were in the highest level—I. This difference between the two groups (the delayed children showing less variability than the normal children) occurs also on other measures.

On the Proportion of Closed Syllables, the normal children show a tremendous range—from no closed syllables for Hildegard to virtually all closed syllables by Joan (0.87). Their mean score, 0.50, suggests that normal children's score will fall along the entire continuum in this regard. Because of this, they are divided into two groups: those that prefer closed syllables (0.50–1.00) and those showing predominantly open syllables, (0–0.49). The delayed children show, on the other hand, more preference for open syllables, which supports the claim made by Renfrew (1966). Their range is more limited—from 0.05 to 0.73—and their mean is only 0.39. Ten of these 15 subjects fall into the group showing preference for open syllables. The fact that five delayed children show closed syllables, however, suggests that this may be a tendency rather than a type.

7.1.2 Results of the Analysis of Homonymy

The issue of the extent of homonymy in children's language is one that draws attention in studies of both normal and language-delayed subjects (c.f., discussion in Chapter 4). The Analysis of Homonymy described in Chapter 4 takes an important step

Table 11. Sounds used by at least one third of all subjects and the number of 15 normal and 15 delayed children who used a sound either: 1) transitionally—(C); 2) to criterion—C; or 3) at least twice the criterion—C* for three word positions of initial, medial, and final

| | Number of subjects and level of frequency | | | | | | |
| | (C) | | C | | C* | | |
Sounds	Normal	Delayed	Normal	Delayed	Normal	Delayed	Total
Initial							
b	0	1	1	2	14	12	30
d	0	0	4	5	11	10	30
m	0	4	9	6	5	3	27
w	2	0	5	6	4	7	24
t	1	2	4	1	4	12	24
h	1	1	6	8	2	1	19
p	1	1	6	4	1	5	18
k	1	2	5	3	3	4	18
n	3	1	5	5	3	0	17
g	0	3	4	2	4	0	13
f	0	1	4	4	1	2	12
s	2	0	3	5	0	0	10
Medial							
b	3	7	5	1	3	1	20
d	2	3	6	4	3	1	19
t	0	7	3	2	1	1	14
m	5	3	2	1	0	1	12
p	0	7	2	1	0	0	10
Final							
t	0	2	6	4	6	3	21
n	2	2	3	3	4	6	20
k	0	1	4	4	6	2	17
p	0	5	7	2	1	0	15
m	5	5	0	3	1	0	14

toward the resolution of this topic by proposing measures in terms of ratios and proportions of the occurrence of Homonymous forms and Homonymous types. Table 13 presents these measures for the 30 subjects of this report.

The normal children have been divided into three groups in terms of their use of homonymy, based on their proportions of Homonymous Types. These groupings are as follows:

A. Low Homonymy   0.00 to 0.09
B. Moderate Homonymy   0.10 to 0.15
C. High Homonymy   0.16 and up

The normal subjects are represented in all three levels but most of them are in the High Homonymy group. These data strongly suggest that the extent of homonymy in normal children's speech will vary tremendously.

The data from the delayed children reveals that there is a smaller range and many more subjects in the group with High Homonymy. These data support, to some extent, the suggestion in Ingram (1976) that these children may evidence more homonymy than normal children. You need to realize, however, that these data suggest only a tendency

because they do not reach statistical significance (c.f., Ingram, 1980), and that some normal children show as much homonymy as their delayed counterparts. Consequently, what is most important is to determine each individual child's own Proportion of Homonymy.

7.1.3 Results of the Substitution Analysis

Even though the two groups of children may use similar sounds (c.f., Section 7.1.1), this does not necessarily mean that their substitutions will be similar. Table 14 presents the Proportion of Matches, broken down into initial, ambisyllabic, and final position, for the 30 children. A low proportion for a child indicates that he or she is not matching the adult sounds often. The data from each group are divided arbitrarily into four groups based on this proportion: I—(0–0.25) Low; II—(0.26–0.50) Moderately Low; III—(0.51–0.75) Moderately High; and IV—(0.76–1.00) High.

We can see that, for both groups, no children fall into the High category, indicating that at this level, the child's acquisition is still undeveloped. What is different for the two groups, however, is their distribution in Group I and III. Only three of the normal children fall into the Low Category, whereas seven of

Table 12. Proportion of Monosyllables and Proportion of Closed Syllables for 15 normal and 15 language-delayed children

Proportion of monosyllables				Proportion of closed syllables			
Normal		Delayed		Normal		Delayed	
I		**II**		Joan	0.87	Tanya	0.73
Daniel	0.95	#9 (girl)	0.79	R	0.82	Ricky	0.71
DeCamp	0.86	Ricky	0.74	Daniel	0.81	Ron	0.71
Jon	0.84	Tanya	0.71	A	0.77	Billy	0.60
Joan	0.81	Adam	0.69	Ruth	0.68	Darren	0.58
Jacob	0.80	John	0.67	Jennifer	0.62	Kevin	0.45
		#6 (boy)	0.64	Jon	0.59	Bill	0.42
II		Kris	0.63			John	0.42
R (boy)	0.78	Ethel I	0.61	Jacob	0.44	#6	0.37
M	0.73	Bill	0.60	M	0.44	#9	0.22
Amy	0.71			Jennika	0.43	Kris	0.22
Molly	0.69	**III**		Molly	0.34	J	0.13
Ruth	0.68	Kevin	0.59	Amy	0.26	Ethel I	0.09
Jennifer	0.67	Ron	0.59	DeCamp	0.20	Adam	0.09
		Darren	0.58	Philip	0.16	Rosie	0.05
III		J	0.53	Hildegard	0.00		
Jennika	0.57	Billy	0.53				
A (boy)	0.53	Rosie	0.52	Mean	0.50	Mean	0.39
Philip	0.48						
Hildegard	0.33	Mean	0.63				
Mean	0.70						

the delayed children do. At the other end, five of the normal children fall into the Moderately High category but only two of the delayed children do. These preliminary results suggest that the kinds of sounds produced by delayed children do not differ as much as the children's ability to match the adult sounds does.

Next, we can look at the individual consonants for both groups and the three syllable positions to get a general idea of which ones are easier to match. Table 15 presents these results for sounds for which at least five subjects in each group attempted. (Each subject had to attempt at least two words with the target sound in them.)

Table 13. The ratios and proportions of Homonymous forms and Homonymous types for 15 normal and 15 language-delayed children

Child	Ratio Forms	Ratio Types	Proportion Forms	Proportion Types	Child	Ratio Forms	Ratio Types	Proportion Forms	Proportion Types
A					**A**				
Jon			0.00	0.00	Ricky	22:1	12:1	0.04	0.08
Jennifer	67:1	27:1	0.02	0.04	**B**				
M	32:1	16:1	0.03	0.06	#6	16:1	8:1	0.06	0.11
R	29:1	13:1	0.03	0.07	Bill	15:1	8:1	0.06	0.12
B					**C**				
Daniel	18:1	8:1	0.05	0.11	Darren	13:1	5:1	0.09	0.18
Hildegard	16:1	7:1	0.06	0.13	Billy	11:1	5:1	0.10	0.18
Jennika	22:1	6:1	0.04	0.14	Tanya	9:1	5:1	0.10	0.18
Molly	11:1	6:1	0.08	0.15	Ethel I	11:1	4:1	0.09	0.19
C					John	8:1	4:1	0.11	0.20
Amy	6:1	4:1	0.14	0.19	Kevin	11:1	4:1	0.09	0.21
Philip	8:1	3:1	0.11	0.23	Rosie	8:1	4:1	0.11	0.21
Ruth	7:1	3:1	0.12	0.23	Ron	10:1	4:1	0.09	0.22
A	7:1	3:1	0.12	0.23	#9	8:1	3:1	0.12	0.26
Jacob	9:1	3:1	0.10	0.25	Kris	7:1	3:1	0.12	0.26
DeCamp	5:1	3:1	0.16	0.28	Adam	6:1	3:1	0.14	0.27
Joan	9:1	2:1	0.10	0.32	J	5:1	2:1	0.16	0.31
		Mean	0.08	0.16			Mean	0.10	0.20

There are at least two aspects of the results in Table 15 that need to be considered in a general overview of children's substitution abilities. First, there is the question of degree of difficulty. In these data, blanks superficially indicate lack of data, but they can also be interpreted as suggestive of difficult sounds because young children will often avoid attempting sounds that they cannot produce (Ferguson and Farwell, 1975). If we interpret avoidance this way, it can be seen that the intervocalic position has the most blanks, suggesting that this is the most difficult syllable position.

To get a general picture of the difficulty of individual segments, consider first just those sounds in Table 15 attempted by both groups. Furthermore, let's say that the two groups find a sound equally difficult if their Proportions of Matches are within 0.25 of each other, and these sounds are called Similar Sounds. Then, the scores for both groups on Similar Sounds can be averaged to provide a gross idea of degree of difficulty. When this is done, the following order of difficulty emerges:

Order of Difficulty of Similar Sounds

Initial		Ambisyllabic		Final	
/d-/	0.66	/-m-/	0.90	/-m/	0.52
/p-/ /t-/ /w-/	0.59	/-k-/	0.42	/-f/	0.50
/k-/	0.27	/-d-/	0.23	/-s/	0.19
/s-/	0.12	/-t-/	0.22	/-n/	0.17
/l-/	0.04			/-z/	0.13
/r-/	0.00			/-l/	0.09
				/-r/	0.09
				/-θ/ /-t/	0.07
				/-d/	0.05

Of particular interest in the data are those sounds that show a proportional difference between the groups that is greater than 0.25. These will be referred to as Different Sounds and are as follows:

Different Sounds

Initial	Normal	Delayed
/m-/	1.00	0.73
/n-/	0.91	0.60
/b-/	1.00	0.60
/g-/	0.86	0.33
/f-/	0.67	0.36
/h-/	0.42	0.77
Final		
/-p/	0.67	0.08
/-k/	0.46	0.07
/-g/	0.43	0.17

These suggest that the following adult English sounds (in their order of increasing difficulty) pose particular problems for language-delayed children: 1) initial nasals 2) initial voiced stops 3) final voiceless stops 4) final velar stops. The only sound that seems easier for language-delayed children than it is for normal children is /h-/.

The second aspect of these data that needs to be considered is the difference between phonetic and substitutional difficulty. This concerns the difference between the ability to articulate a sound and the ability to produce it when necessary within a particular linguistic system. It may be (e.g., Locke, in press) that there is a universal hierarchy in the articulatory ability for a child to produce different sounds, but the ability to acquire a particular sound within a lan-

Table 14. Proportion of Matches for 15 normal and 15 language-delayed subjects for initial (I), ambisyllabic (A), and final (F) consonants[a]

	Normal	Syllable position				Delayed	Syllable position		
Child	I	A	F	Total	Child	I	A	F	Total
I					**I**				
Philip	0.23	0.33	0.00	0.14	J	0.29	0.14	0.00	0.15
A	0.24	0.27	0.13	0.21	Rosie	0.31		0.00	0.17
Hildegard	0.67	(0.00)	0.00	0.25	Kevin	0.13	0.17	0.27	0.19
					Ron	0.08	0.33	0.30	0.21
II					Ethel	0.36	0.20	0.00	0.22
Jennika	0.56	(0.00)	0.00	0.28	Darren	0.27	0.25	0.00	0.23
Amy	0.50	(0.00)	0.00	0.29	#9	0.42	(1.00)	0.00	0.25
Jacob	0.55	0.50	0.09	0.33					
Ruth	0.35	0.46	0.33	0.38	**II**				
Molly	0.56	(0.00)	0.14	0.41	Tanya	0.29	0.57	0.14	0.29
R (boy)	0.29	0.71	0.53	0.46	Bill	0.40	0.44	0.24	0.34
Joan	0.57	0.80	0.29	0.49	Kris	0.40	(1.00)	0.00	0.36
					Adam	0.64	(0.00)	0.08	0.37
III					John	0.47	0.75	0.27	0.43
Daniel	0.31		0.80	0.52	Billy	0.60	0.83	0.08	0.44
M (girl)	0.67	0.00	0.30	0.53					
Jon	0.67		0.33	0.56	#6	0.83	1.00	0.09	0.54
Jennifer	0.75	0.78	0.27	0.57	Ricky	0.67	0.80	0.54	0.64
DeCamp	1.00	(1.00)	0.00	0.60					
			Mean	0.40				Mean	0.32

[a]Results from 4 or fewer subjects for any position are placed within parentheses.

Table 15. The Proportion of Matches for English consonants for 15 normal and 15 language-delayed children for initial, intervocalic, and final syllable positions[a]

Target Sound	Initial		Intervocalic		Final	
	Normal	Delayed	Normal	Delayed	Normal	Delayed
/m/	1.00	0.73	1.00	0.80	0.57	0.46
/n/	0.91	0.60		0.50	0.07	0.27
/ŋ/	////[b]	////				0.38
/p/	0.55	0.60		0.75	0.67	0.08
/b/	1.00	0.60	1.00			
/t/	0.58	0.60	0.20	0.43	0.07	0.07
/d/	0.64	0.67	0.40	0.25	0.09	0.00
/k/	0.20	0.33	0.33	0.50	0.46	0.07
/g/	0.86	0.33			0.43	0.17
/tʃ/						
/dʒ/						
/f/	0.67	0.36			0.60	0.40
/θ/					0.00	0.14
/s/	0.23	0.00			0.31	0.07
/ʃ/						0.13
/v/						0.00
/ð/		0.00				
/z/					0.25	0.00
/ʒ/	////	////				
/w/	0.58	0.60			////	////
/j/					////	////
/r/	0.00	0.00			0.07	0.08
/l/	0.00	0.07			0.00	0.17
/h/	0.42	0.77			////	////

[a]At least five subjects had to attempt each sound for it to be included.
[b]//// indicates places where the target sound does not occur in English.

guage will depend on the linguistic circumstances of that sound within a particular phonological system.

This can be demonstrated in our data for final [t]. Based on the analysis in Section 7.1.1, [t] is the easiest or one of the easiest sounds for children to produce in final position. At the same time, the data in the Substitution Analysis presented in Table 16 shows that /-t/ is matched by only 7% of the children who attempt it. In other words, /-t/ is one of the more difficult English sounds to acquire. The reason for this is the complexity of contexts in which English /-t/ appears. For example, it occurs not just at the end of stressed syllables ("cat," "hat"), an optimal place, but also at the end of unstressed syllables ("basket," "cigarette"). Also, it occurs in a variety of clusters, for example, "bent," "fast," "belt." The particular distributional characteristic of /-t/ also makes it a difficult sound to acquire. The degree of difficulty of any sound, therefore, varies from language to language, dependent on that language's phonological system.

Last, we can look at the main substitutions used by the normal and delayed subjects for the English consonant system. Table 16 presents those that occur at least in two subjects within either the normal or delayed groups. Those substitutions that differ between the normal and delayed children are circled.

It is not surprising that the delayed children show more substitution because their Proportions of Matches are lower (Table 15). When grouped, they give a general idea of the kinds and frequency of use of the substitutions found in the data from these 30 subjects. The next section describes in more detail the extent and types of differences that occur.

7.1.4 Results of the Phonological Process Analysis

Ingram (1976, 1978) observed that children with phonological delay do not exhibit unique or different processes as much as the persistence or use of processes that normal children rarely use, or lose at an early age. In this data, processes were determined for those substitutions in Table 16 according to the partial analysis described in Chapter 6. Recall that this is a strict procedure that only isolates the more frequent processes in the data. Table 17 presents a summary of the processes that were used: 1) by both groups; 2) by delayed subjects only; 3) by normal subjects only; 4) by neither group. Also, the table indicates which adult sounds were affected for each group.

Notice first of all that the majority of processes are used by both groups. Within these, there are some differences in the range of sounds affected. For

Table 16. Substitutions used by at least 2 subjects within a group, for sounds shown in Table 15, by 15 normal and 15 language-delayed children[a]

Target Sound	Initial		Intervocalic		Final	
	Normal	Delayed	Normal	Delayed	Normal	Delayed
/m/	—	ⓑ(2)	—	—	ø(2)	ø(7)
/n/	—	ⓓ(3)	—	ø⃝(3) ?⃝(2)	ø(12) m(2)	ø(11)
/ŋ/	////[b]	////			—	ⓝ(4) ø⃝(2)
/p/	b(5)	b(3) ⓣ,ⓓ(2)	ⓑ(2)	—	ø(3)	ø(10) ⓣ(2)
/b/	—	ⓟ,ⓣ,ⓓ(2)	—	—	—	
/t/	d(5)	d(3)	d(2)	ø⃝(3) ?⃝, d(2)	ø(12) ⓟ(2)	ø(11) ?⃝(2)
/d/	ⓖ(4)	ⓣ(2)	ø(3)	ø(5)	ø(10) t(2)	ø(12) t(2)
/k/	ⓖ(6) ⓓ(4)	ⓣ(8)	ⓖ(3)	—	ø(5) ⓣ(3)	ø(13)
/g/	—	ⓓ(7)			ⓚ(2)	ø⃝(4)
/f/	—	ⓟ(4)			—	ø⃝(3)
/θ/	—	ⓣ(2) ⓕ(2)			ⓣ(2)	ø⃝(5)
/s/	ø(8) ʃ⃝(2)	ø(11) ⓣ(5)			ø(8) ʃ⃝(2)	ø(13)
/ʃ/	ø⃝(2)	—			—	ø⃝(5)
/v/	—	—			—	ø⃝(5)
/z/	—	—			ø(5)	ø(11)
/w/	ø(5)	ø(3)			////	////
/r/	ø(11) w(5)	ø(10) w(10)			ø(14)	ø(11)
/l/	ø(10)	ø(11) ⓦ(5)			ø(14)	ø(10)
/h/	ø(7)	ø(2)			////	////

[a](—) indicates no cases of substitution, blanks indicate target sound not attempted. Sounds that differ between the two groups are circled. The number of subjects showing each substitution is shown in parentheses.

[b]//// indicates places where the target sound does not occur in English.

the five processes affecting the deletion of final consonants, the normal subjects show four affected segments whereas the delayed children show ten. The frequency of the other affected segments for the shared processes are more comparable.

The data in Table 17 reveal that five of the processes found in the data are unique to the delayed subjects and three to the normal children. Because of the diversity of sampling procedures and the generality of the analysis, not too much importance should be placed on the differences. For example, the processes listed "processes not used" occurred in the data, but not in enough lexical types to meet the strict frequency criteria of Chapter 6. Several of these occur for affricates, a small class that is not particularly frequent in the words of young children. Even so, the data do suggest areas for future examination in explaining processes that may characterize language delay. In another study on the development of fricatives in normal and delayed children (c.f., Ingram, 1978) it was also observed that Stop-

ping and Apicalization were more characteristic of the delayed subjects. These data provide at least an overview of the range of occurrence of the most basic processes used by children.

7.2 A PROFILE OF PHONOLOGICAL DEVELOPMENT

As more data are analyzed by the procedures described, and as the procedures are developed and expanded, we should be able to determine norms that may be used to construct reliable profiles of children's phonological development. Eventually, these can be reduced to a single Profile Sheet on which we can place our data for the purposes of comparison. A first approximation of such a Profile Sheet is provided in Sample Analysis 7.1. It undoubtedly will be changed and elaborated as future research adds to our understanding of phonological development. Also, because the samples used here cover very young normal children, confirmation will

Table 17. Twenty-seven phonological processes and affected segments for substitutions in Table 16 that are used by: 1) normal and delayed subjects; 2) delayed subjects only; 3) normal subjects only; 4) neither group[a]

Phonological Processes	Affected target sounds	
	Normal	Delayed
1. Used by both groups		
(1) FCD of nasals	-n(5)	-n(5) -m(2)
(2) FCD of voiced stops	-d(4)	-d(5) -g(3)
(3) FCD of voiceless stops	-t(7)	-k(9) -t(8) -p(3)
(5) FCD of voiceless fricatives	-s(4)	-s(7) -θ(3) -ʃ(2)
(6) Liquid cluster reduction	C/r/(7) C/1/(6)	C/r/(5) C/1/(4)
(8) /s/C cluster reduction	/s/C(3)	/s/C(9)
(11) Reduplication	(4 subjects)	(6 subjects)
(13) Fronting of velars	-k(4) k-(2)	k-(5) g-(5)
(15) Stopping of voiced fricatives	ð-(2)	ð-(2)
(17) Liquid gliding	r-(4)	r-(5) 1-(3)
(18) Vocalization	-ļ(2) ɾ(2)	-ļ(2)
2. Delayed only		
(4) FCD of voiced fricatives		-z(6)
(7) Cluster reduction of nasals		NC voiceless(2) NC voiced(2)
(10) Unstressed syllable deletion		(6 subjects)
(14) Stopping of initial voiceless fricatives		f-(3) s-(3)
(22) Apicalization		f-(2)
3. Normal only		
(21) Deletion of initial consonants	h-(4) w-(2) s-(2)	
(24) Velar assimilation	d-(2)	
(26) Voicing	k-(7) p-(4) t-(4) -k-(2) s-(2)	
4. Processes not used		
(9) Reduction of disyllables		
(12) Fronting of palatals		
(16) Stopping of affricates		
(19) Denasalization		
(20) Deaffrication		
(23) Labialization		
(25) Labial assimilation		
(27) Devoicing of final consonants		

[a]Only affected segments for at least two subjects within a group are shown. Number of subjects using each process are given in parentheses.

be needed to cover development after age 2. In any case, the present form at least will enable you to get a gross idea of how a child's development compares to that of the young 2-year-old.

Sample Analysis 7.1 and 7.2 are Profile Sheets of Jennika and R, respectively. The data have been entered by simply inserting the relevant numbers, circling level of performances, and crossing out sounds not used and entering those that are. For phonological processes, those affecting two or more segments are entered, with no normative judgments made.

These two profile sheets help isolate the similarities and differences between these two children. On Articulation Scores, they are far apart, with Jennika being a little below the mean, while R has more sounds than the normal 2-year-old, although he is only slightly beyond. When looking at the phonetic inventories, we see that R has the expected sounds, except for the striking case where initial [f] is missing. As the Substitution Analysis revealed, R has a great deal of difficulty with that sound. Clinically, it would be a prime candidate for remediation.

On the syllables scores, C and D, we see that they both use a low proportion of monosyllables, yet differ in the use of closed syllables. R is quite good at employing these whereas Jennika still uses a number of open ones. The last two measures both show differences. R used a High degree of homonymy whereas Jennika comes out Moderate on this measure. They are closer together on Proportion of Matches, although our divisions place R in the Low group and Jennika in the Moderately Low Group.

7.3 CONCLUDING REMARKS

In some ways, the extent of data that have been accumulated and researched in the area of phonological development is formidable. There are various cross-sectional studies, and individual studies of children, both longitudinally and based on single samples. At the same time, the utility of these data is somewhat limited because of the diversity of methodologies and analytic procedures. This is particularly true when we consider the information of use to the practicing clinician or researcher who wishes to gain insight into the system of a specific child. It is hoped that the procedures outlined in this book and the norms provided in this one are at least one step, however tentative, in that direction.

REFERENCES

Abrahamsen, A. A. 1977. Child Language: An Interdisciplinary Guide to Theory and Research. University Park Press, Baltimore.

Adams, N. 1972. Unpublished phonological diary of son Philip from 1;7 to 2;3.

Allen, G., and Hawkins, S. 1978. The development of phonological rhythm. In: A. Bell and J. B. Hooper (eds.), Syllables and Segments, pp. 173–185. Elsevier North Holland Publishing Co., New York.

Bloom, L., and Lahey, M. 1978. Language Development and Language Disorders. John Wiley and Sons, Inc., New York.

Brown, R. 1973. A First Language: The Early Stages. Harvard University Press, Cambridge, Mass.

DeCamp, L. 1946. Learning to talk. Am. Speech. 21:23–28.

Ferguson, 1966.

Ferguson, C. 1968. Contrastive analysis and language development. In: Monograph Series on Language and Linguistics, 21: 101–112. Georgetown University, Washington, D.C.

Ferguson, C., and Farwell, C. 1975. Words and sounds in early language acquisition. Language 51:419–439.

Ferguson, C., and Garnica, O. 1975. Theories of phonological development. In: E. Lenneberg and E. Lenneberg (eds.), Foundations of Language Development, pp. 153–180, Vol. 1. Academic Press, Inc., New York.

Foulke, K., and Stinchfield, S. 1929. The speech development of four infants under two years of age. Pedagogical Seminary 36:140–171.

Grammont. 1902. Observations sur le language des enfants. In: Mélanges Linguistiques Offerts à M. Antoine Meillet, Paris, Klincksieck, pp. 61–82.

Grunwell, P. 1975. Therapeutic guidelines from linguistics—a case study. Unpublished paper.

Grunwell, P. 1977. The analysis of phonological disability in children. Unpublished doctoral dissertation, University of Reading, England.

Hills, E. 1914. The speech of a child two years of age. Dialect Notes 4:84–100.

Hinckley, A. C. 1915. A case of retarded speech development. Pedagogical Seminary 22:121–146.

Hodson, B., and Paden, E. Phonological processes which characterize unintelligible and intelligible speech in early childhood. J. Speech Hear. Disord. In press.

Holmes, U. 1927. The phonology of an English-speaking child. Am. Speech 2:219–225.

Ingram, D. 1974. Phonological rules in young children. J. Child Lang. 1:49–64.

Ingram, D. 1976. Phonological Disability in Children. Edward Arnold. Publishers Ltd., London.

Ingram, D. 1978. The production of word-initial fricatives and affricates in normal and linguistically deviant children. In: A. Caramazza and E. Zuriff (eds.), The Acquisition and Breakdown of Language, pp. 63–85. Johns Hopkins University Press, Baltimore.

Ingram, D. 1978. The role of the syllable in phonological development. In: A. Bell and J. Hooper (eds.), Syllables and Segments, pp. 143–155. Elsevier North Holland Publishing Co., New York.

Ingram, D. 1979. Phonological patterns in the speech of young children. In: P. Fletcher and M. Garman (eds.), Language Acquisition, pp. 133–148. Cambridge University Press, Cambridge.

Ingram, D. 1980. A comparative study of phonological development in normal and linguistically delayed children. Paper presented at the Symposium on Research in Child Language Disorders, June, Madison, Wis.

Ingram, D. The Acquisition of a First Language. In preparation.

Ingram, D., Christensen, L., Veach, S., and Webster, B. The acquisition of word initial fricatives and affricates in English by children between two and six. In: J. Kavanaugh, G. Yeni-Komshian and C. Ferguson (eds.), Child Phonology: Data and Theory. Academic Press, New York. In Press.

Jordan, J. 1976. The development of a procedure for the description of phonological processes in a child with multiple misarticulations. Unpublished paper, University of Wisconsin, Madison, Wis.

Klein, H. 1977. The relationship between perceptual strategies and productive strategies in learning the phonology of early lexical items, Unpublished doctoral dissertation, Columbia University, New York.

Ladefoged, P. 1975. A Course in Phonetics. Harcourt Brace Jovanovich, New York.

Leopold, W. 1947. Speech Development of a Bilingual Child: A Linguist's Record, Vol. 2. Northwestern University Press, Evanston, Ill.

Leopold, W. 1952. Bibliography of Child Language. Northwestern University Press, Evanston, Ill.

Locke, J. The prediction of child speech errors: Implications for a theory of acquisition. In: G. Yeni-Komshian, J. Kavanaugh, and C. Ferguson (eds.), Child Phonology: Data and Theory. Academic Press, Inc., New York. In press.

McCarthy, D. 1954. Language development in children. In: L. Carmichael (ed.), Manual of Child Psychology, pp. 492–630. 2nd Ed. John Wiley & Sons, Inc., New York.

Menn, L. 1971. Phonotactic rules in beginning speech. Lingua 26:225–251.

Menn, L. 1976. Pattern, control and contrast in beginning speech: A case study in the development of word form and word function. Unpublished doctoral dissertation, University of Illinois.

Priestly, T. M. S. On homonymy in child phonology. J. Child Lang. In press.

Renfrew, C. E. 1966. Persistence of the open syllable in defective articulation. J. Speech Hear. Disord. 31:370–373.

Schwartz, R. G., Leonard, L. B., Wilcox, M. J., and Folger, K. 1980. Again and again: reduplication in child phonology. J. Child Lang. 7:75–88.

Scollon, 1976. Conversations With a One-Year-Old. The University Press of Hawaii, Honolulu.

Shriberg, L., and Kwiatkowski, J. 1980. Procedure for Natural Process Analyses (NPA) of Continuous Speech Samples: NPA Application Manual. John Wiley & Sons, Inc., New York.

Slobin, D. 1972. Leopold's Bibliography of Child Language. Indiana University Press, Bloomington, Ind.

Smith, N. 1973. The Acquisition of Phonology: A Case Study. Cambridge University Press, Cambridge.

Stampe, D. 1969. The acquisition of phonetic representation. Papers from Chicago Linguistic Society, 5th Regional Meeting, Chicago, Ill.

Stoel-Gammon, 1980. Phonological processes in the speech of Down's syndrome children. Paper presented at the Symposium on Research on Child Language Disorders, June 6, 7, Madison, Wis.

Templin, M. 1957. Certain Language Skills in Children: Their Development and Interrelationships. Institute of Child Welfare Monograph 26. The University of Minnesota Press, Minneapolis.

Velten, J. 1943. The growth of phonemic and lexical patterns in infant language. Language 19:281–292.

Vihman, M. 1979. Homonymy and the organization of early vocabulary. Paper presented at the Stanford Child Language Research Forum in April. Stanford, Cal.

Weiner, F. 1979. Phonological Process Analysis. University Park Press, Baltimore.

EXPERIMENTAL PROFILE SHEET

Child's name and age ___Jennika 1;5___

I. **Phonetic Analysis**

    A. _31_   Articulation Score (range of sample 18 to 49, with a mean of 40) Circle one:

        1. (Below mean)   2. At or above mean   3. Beyond range

    B. **Basic Phonetic Inventories**

       initial   medial   final

       (m) n   m   (m) n

       (b)(d) g   (b)(d)   p (t) k

       (p) t k   (p)(t)   (ʧ)

       f s h

       (w)

    C. _0.57_ Proportion of Monosyllables

        I. High 0.80–1.00   II. Moderate 0.60–0.79   III. (Low) 0.00–0.59

    D. _0.43_ Proportion of Closed Syllables (mean 0.50)

        Higher 0.51–1.00   (Lower) 0.00–0.49

II. **Analysis of Homonymy**

    _0.14_ Proportion of Homonymous Types

        A. Low 0.00–0.09   B. (Moderate) 0.10–0.15   C. High 0.16 or higher

III. **Substitution Analysis**

    _0.29_ Proportion of Matches

        I. Low 0.00–0.25   (II. Moderately Low) 0.26–0.50

        III. Moderately High 0.51–0.75   IV. High 0.76–1.00

IV. **Phonological Processes Analysis**

    _9_ Number of processes   _10_ Number of affected segments

    Most general processes (and affected segments):

    Deletion of Final Consonants /-t/ /-g/; /-r/

    Fronting of Palatal /k-/ /k-/ /-k/

    Reduplication

EXPERIMENTAL PROFILE SHEET

Child's name and age   R 3;11

I. **Phonetic Analysis**
  A. _52_ Articulation Score (range of sample 18 to 49, with a mean of 40) Circle one:

    1. **Below mean**   2. **At or above mean**   (3. **Beyond range**)

  B. **Basic Phonetic Inventories**

initial	medial	final
(m) (n)	(m) (n)	(m) n
(b) (d) (g)	b (d) ʒ	p t k
(p) (t) (k)	(p) t	(f) (s)
f (s) (h)	(s) (j)	
(w)		

  C. _0.59_ Proportion of Monosyllables
    I. High 0.80–1.00   II. Moderate 0.60–0.79   III. (Low) 0.00–0.59
  D. _0.71_ Proportion of Closed Syllables (mean 0.50)
    (Higher) 0.51–1.00   Lower 0.00–0.49

II. **Analysis of Homonymy**
    _0.22_ Proportion of Homonymous Types
    A. Low 0.00–0.09   B. Moderate 0.10–0.15   (C. High) 0.16 or higher

III. **Substitution Analysis**
    _0.21_ Proportion of Matches
    I. (Low) 0.00–0.25   II. Moderately Low 0.26–0.50
    III. Moderately High 0.51–0.75   IV. High 0.76–1.00

IV. **Phonological Processes Analysis**
    _8_ Number of processes   _7_ Number of affected segments
    Most general processes (and affected segments):

    Reduction of Consonant Clusters C/r/-; /s/C-
    Stopping of: Fricatives /f-/; Liquids /l-/
    Vocalization /-l/ /r/
    Devoicing /-b, -d/

APPENDIX   A

Sample Analysis Forms

LEXICON SHEET

Child's name and age _____

types		types		types		types	
lexical	phonetic	lexical	phonetic	lexical	phonetic	lexical	phonetic

SAMPLE

CONSONANT INVENTORY SHEET

Lexical Types   Child's name and age _____

_____ initial   _____ ambisyllabic   _____ final

b			d			dʒ			g		

p			t			tʃ			k		

v			z			ʒ			ð		

f			s						θ		

w			l			r			h		

									vowel		

m			n						ŋ		

CONSONANT INVENTORY SHEET
Phonetic Forms   Child's name and age _____

_____ initial   _____ medial   _____ final

SAMPLE

ITEM AND REPLICA SHEET

Child's name and age _____

Child's Phonetic Inventory

Word initial segments

m		n					
p	b	t	d	tʃ	dʒ	k	g
f	v	θ	ð	ʃ		Vowel	
		s	z				
w		r		j		h	
		l					

Child's Substitutions

Syllable initial consonants

Word medial consonants

m		n				ŋ	
p	b	t	d	tʃ	dʒ		
f	v	θ	ð	ʃ			
		s	z				
w		r				h	
		l					

consonants

Word final consonants

m		n				ŋ	
p	b	t	d	tʃ	dʒ	k	g
f	v	θ	ð	ʃ	ʒ		
		s	z				
		r		ɾ			
		l		ḷ			

Syllable final consonants

CHILD SYLLABLE SHEET

Child's name and age _____

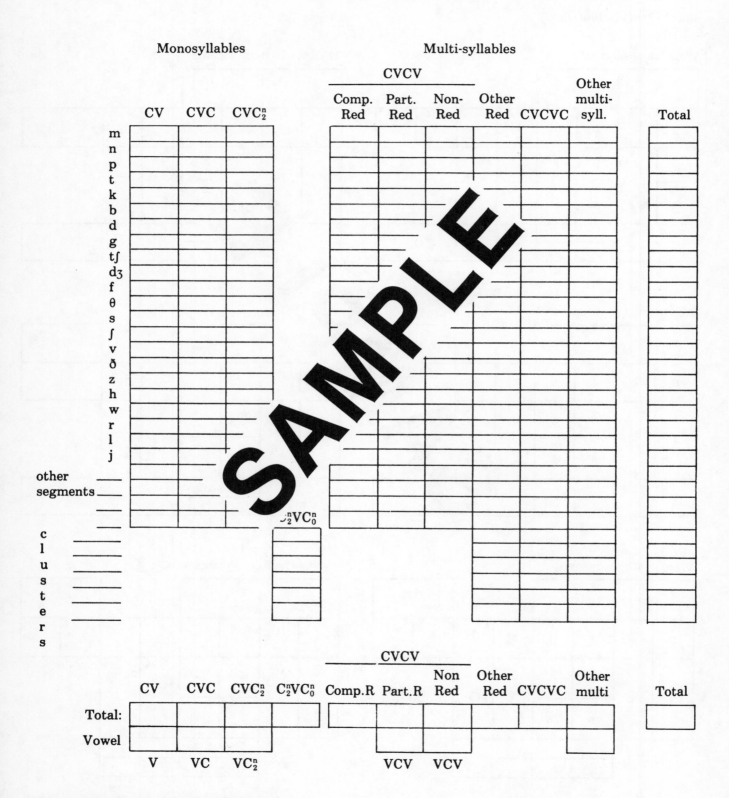

HOMONYMY SHEET

Child's name and age _____

Homonymous forms	Homonymous types	No. of types
1. [ ]	_____	_____
2. [ ]	_____	_____
3. [ ]	_____	_____
4. [ ]	_____	_____
5. [ ]	_____	_____
6. [ ]	_____	_____
7. [ ]	_____	_____
8. [ ]	_____	_____
9. [ ]	_____	_____
10. [ ]	_____	_____
11. [ ]	_____	_____
12. [ ]	_____	_____
13. [ ]	_____	_____
14. [ ]	_____	_____
15. [ ]	_____	_____

Summary of data

_____ total number of hom_____ (A)   _____ number of homonymous types (D)

_____ total number of phonetic forms (B)   _____ number of lexical types (E)

_____ total number of nonhomonymous forms (C)   _____ number of nonhomonymous types (F)

Calculation of Extent of Homonymy

1. Ratio of Homonymous forms
C:A _____:_____ _____:1

2. Ratio of Homonymous types
F:D _____:_____ _____:1

3. Proportion of Homonymous forms

_____

4. Proportion of Homonymous types

_____

PHONOLOGICAL PROCESSES SHEET

Child's name and age _____

Syllable Structure Processes

Deletion of Final Consonants (FCD):

(1) nasals: /-m/ /-n/ /-ŋ/   (3) voiceless stops: /-p/ /-t/ /-k/

_____ _____ _____   _____ _____ _____

(2) voiced stops: /-b/ /-d/ /-g/   (4) voiced fricatives: /-v/ /-ð/ /-ʒ/ /-dʒ/

_____ _____ _____   _____ _____ _____ _____

(5) voiceless fricatives: /-f/ /-θ/ /-s/ /-ʃ/ /-tʃ/

_____ _____ _____ _____ _____

Reduction of Consonant Clusters (CR):

	(6) Liquids			√Cvless	(8) /s/ clusters
	C/l/-	C/r/-			/s/C-
reduced to C	_____	_____		_____	_____
C deleted	_____	_____		_____	_____
cluster deleted	_____	_____		_____	_____
Total	_____	_____		_____	_____

Syllable Deletion

(9) Reduction of Disyllables (RD) _____ (10) Unstressed syllable deletionUSD) _____

(11) Reduplication _____

Substitution Processes

Fronting   (12) of Palatals (PF)   (13) of Velars (VF)

syllable position	/ʃ/	/ʒ/	/tʃ/	/dʒ/		/k/	/g/	/ŋ/
initial	___	___	___	___		___	___	___
intervocalic	___	___	___	___		___	___	___
final	___	___	___	___		___	___	___

Stopping (S)   (14) of Initial Voiceless Fricatives   (15) of Initial Voiced Fricatives

/f/	/θ/	/s/	/ʃ/		/v/	/ð/	/z/	/ʒ/
___	___	___	___		___	___	___	___

(16) of Affricates

/tʃ/	/dʒ/
___	___

SAMPLE

Simplification of Liquids and Nasals

(17) Liquid Gliding (LG))

    substitutes   substitutes

/r-/   [w] _____   [j] _____   /-r-/   [w] _____   [j] _____

/l-/   [w] _____   [j] _____   /-l-/   [w] _____   [j] _____

(18) Vocalization (V):

/ɾ/   [ ] _____   [ ] _____   [ ] _____   [ ] _____

/ḷ/   [ ] _____   [ ] _____   [ ] _____   [ ] _____

(19) Denasalization (DN):

	initial	intervocalic	final	total
/m/	_____	_____	_____	_____
/n/	_____	_____	_____	_____
/ŋ/		_____	_____	_____

Other Substitution Processes

Process	Target	...le position
_____	/ /	_____
_____	/ /	_____
_____	/	_____
_____	/]	_____
_____	[ ]	_____
_____	[ ]	_____
_____	[ ]	_____
_____	[ ]	_____

Assimilation Processes

Process	Sounds	Change	Environment
_____	/ /	[ ]	_____
_____	/ /	[ ]	_____
_____	/ /	[ ]	_____
_____	/ /	[ ]	_____
_____	/ /	[ ]	_____
_____	/ /	[ ]	_____
_____	/ /	[ ]	_____
_____	/ /	[ ]	_____

SUMMARY SHEET

Child's name and age _____

| Sample size | lexical types: _____ | phonetic types: _____ | phonetic tokens: _____ | phonetic forms: _____ |

Phonetic Analysis   Articulation Score _____

Total Number of Sounds _____   Criterion of Frequency _____   ($\overline{2} = \overline{25}$)
word initial _____   word medial _____   word final _____

syllable types: most frequent: _____   Proportion of: _____   Monosyllables _____   Closed syllables

Analysis of Homonymy
Ratio of Homonymous forms _____:1   Homony_____ ____:1
Proportion of Homonymous forms _____   Homor_____ _____

Substitution Analysis

	m	n	ŋ	p	b	t	d	k	g	tʃ	dʒ	f	θ		z	ʒ	w	j	r	l	h	
I			▦													▦						
A																						
F																	▦	▦	▦		▦	

Proportion of Data _____ (/67) and M_____ (/) Acquired sounds _____

Phonological Process Analysis

_____ Processes _____ Affected Segments

FINAL [CONSONANT] DELETION

RED[UCTION OF CO]NSONANT CLUSTERS

S[YLLABLE DE]LETION AND REDUPLICATION

FRO[NTI]NG OF PALATALS AND VELARS

STOPPING OF FRICATIVES AND AFFRICATES

SIMPLIFICATION OF LIQUIDS AND NASALS

OTHER PROCESSES

0.0–0.20   0.21–0.49   0.50–0.79   0.80–.100

APPENDIX *B*

Organization of Phonological Samples for D 2;8 (26)

B.1. DISCUSSION OF THE ANALYSIS

Step 1

Not necessary, because utterances are already numbered. Note that utterances 164 and 167 are imitations. Also, note that utterances 146, 147, 152, 160, 161, 165 contain revised transcriptions in that they have places where one transcription is shown above another, e.g., #152, [$\frac{hiz}{its}$]. Because the higher transcription is made on the second transcription, it is considered the more correct and put on the Lexicon Sheet instead of the lower one.

Step 2

Appendix B.2 contains the entries as they would appear on cards with words listed in their order of appearance in the data and showing the num-

bers of utterances in which they occur. Notice that contractions like "there's" are listed as a single word.

Step 3

Appendix B.2 also shows the numbering of the words within individual letters according to their alphabetical order. These numbers are shown to the left of each word.

Step 4

The child's productions of the words listed on the cards have been placed onto the Lexicon Sheet labeled *Appendix B.3*. Diacritic marks have been deleted, such as the velarization shown on the [l] in *apple*. The frequency of occurrence of repeated phonetic forms is indicated in parentheses.

Appendix B.2. Lexical entries and utterance numbers for data in Table 4

A 1. a. 144, 147, 148, 149
150, 155, 159
2. airplane 144
3. alligator 146
4. apple 149, 150

B 3. boat 148, 158
5. brat 155
6. bus 156
2. birthday 160, 161
1. bed 163
4. boy 164

C 3. clown 159
1. cake 160, 160, 161
2. choo choo 166, 167

D doctor 162

G 1. girl 147
2. grandma 152, 153, 154

H 3. he's 152, 153
1. have 160, 161
2. here 161

I 3. is 146, 147, 148, 149, 164
1. I'll 161
2. in 163

N no 161

O on 161

S sick 164

T 1. that 145, 160, 161
6. this 146, 147, 148, 149
2. the 146, 156, 158, 162, 163, 16
4. there's 154, 155, 156, 158
7. too 158
3. there 165
5. these 162
8. train 165

W 2. work 151
1. want 160

LEXICON SHEET

Lexicon Sheet for D based on data in Table 4

Child's name and age D 2;8 (26)

lexical	phonetic	lexical	phonetic	lexical	phonetic	lexical	phonetic
	types		*types*		*types*		*types*
A. a	æʔ—	O. on	—ɔn—				
	—i—	S. sick	*—sɪk				
	—ʒ—(3x)	T. that	æ				
	ʌ—(2x)		—dæt—(2x)				
airplane	—ɛʒpweɪn	the	—dɪ				
alligator	—bægeʒr		—dʌ—(4x)				
apple	—æpʍl(2x)		—dʒ—				
B. bed	—bɛd	there	dɛʒ—				
birthday	—baɪtdeɪ(2x)	there's	dɛʒz—(4x)				
boat	—boɒt—	these	diz—				
	—boɒt	this	dɪs—(4x)				
boy	*bɔɪ—	too	—tʊ				
brat	—rʒet	train	—tʃeɪn				
bus	—bʌs	W. want	want—				
C. cake	—keɪt(2x)	work	wɒk				
	—keɪk—						
choochoo	tʃʊtʃʊ						
	*tʃʊtʃʊ						
clown	—kwaɒn						
D. doctor	—daktʒr						
G. girl	—gɔwʒ						
grandma	—gwʒema(3x)						
H. have	—hæv—						
	—hæ—						
here	—hiʒ						
he's	hiz—(2x)						
I. I'll	—ʒl—						
in	ɪn—						
is	ɪz—(4x)						
	*—ɪz—						
N. no	no—						

APPENDIX C

Phonetic Analysis of Data for R 3; 11

C.1. DISCUSSION OF THE ANALYSIS

Step 1

The recording of R's phonetic forms is shown in Appendices C.2, C.3, and C.4 for initial, medial, and final word positions, respectively. Note that it doesn't really matter which boxes are used for the insertion of particular segments. Here, the far left columns have been used for labials, the next one for alveolars, the third for palatals, and the far right for velars and glottals. This can be varied according to each individual child's data. For initial segments, two boxes were needed for [t] because of the number of disyllables. Also, homonymous forms have been circled in C.2 so they are noticeable for the Analysis of Homonymy to be done in Chapter 4. Phonetic forms from the same lexical type have been placed within braces, for example, [tait] and [dait] for "light" under final [-t].

Step 2

In this step the syllabic shapes of R's phonetic forms are recorded on the Child Syllable Sheet, taken from Appendix C.2. Here, Appendix C.5 shows these data recorded. There are a total of 88 phonetic forms.

Step 3

Next, we count the frequency of the various consonants and enter this onto the Item and Replica Sheet. Remember that the phonetic forms are first for each sound, and then the lexical types. For example, for word initial [n], there are six phonetic forms [nan] [num] [næn] [naɒk] [nænʌ]

[næno], and seven lexical types because [nan] occurs for three different lexical types, but [næn] and [nan] both represent just one lexical type. Notice that for medial [rs], there is no box on the Item and Replica Sheet, so it is entered in an open space (c.f., Appendix C.6).

Step 4

We can now calculate the Criterion of Phonetic Frequency. First, enter the number of phonetic types, forms, and tokens, and lexical types onto the Summary Sheet (c.f., Appendix C.7). Next, add the number of lexical types and phonetic forms, and divide by 2. Here, this will give us 90 and 88 or 178 divided by 2 for 89. This is divided by 25 to yield 3.56 or *4* as the Criterion of Frequency. This is shown on Appendix C.7.

Step 5

We can now determine R's frequent segments. Returning to the Item and Replica Sheet, we circle all the sounds entered that occur four or more times, that is, those that meet our criterion. Remember that when two numbers are shown, for example, 5/4 for initial [k], we use the lower number, in this case 4. Next, we put those sounds in parentheses that are transitional. Table 5 indicates that sounds occurring two or three times are transitional when the Criterion of Frequency is 4. Last, we star sounds once for each time they meet the criterion, except for the first time. Initial [p], for example, occurs in 10 phonetic forms, and 4 into 10 goes 2, minus 1, equals once beyond criterion. It is shown as p*. Other starred sounds are initial [t] 3 times,

[d] once, [h] once, and [s] once, and final [t] and [k] once each (c.f., Appendix C.6).

Next, the sounds that are circled or in parentheses are summarized on the Summary Sheet. These are taken from Appendix C.6 for R and shown on the Summary Sheet labeled *Appendix C.7*.

Step 6

In the last step, we determine some measures for R's phonetic ability. In the first one, we count up the number of sounds that reach criterion and that are transitional. For R, the Total Number of Sounds is 18(9).

Next, we calculate the Articulation Score. For R, this is as follows:

word initial			word medial		
3 × 5 (p*, t***,			3 × 0		= 0
d*, s*, h*)	=	15	2 × 3 (b, t, g)		= 6
2 × 6 (m, n, b, k,			1 × 6 (m, n, p, d,		
g, w)	=	12	s, j)		= 6
1 × 0	=	0			12
		27			

word final		
3 × 2 (t*, k*)	=	6
2 × 2 (p, n)	=	4
1 × 3 (m, f, s)	=	3
		13

for a total of *52*. This is entered on the Summary Sheet.

Last, we do the counts for syllables. The most frequent syllable types are CVC 37, and CV 15. The Proportion of Monosyllables is obtained by dividing the number of monosyllables (52) by the number of phonetic forms (88) for 0.59. The Proportion of Closed Syllables is the number of CV and CVC syllables (52) divided by the number of CVC syllables (37) for 0.71.

Comparison to Jennika

Chapter 7, Section 7.2, returns to these two sets of data for a more detailed comparison. For now, we can make some general observations. Overall, R is more advanced than Jennika. He shows a much higher articulation score, and twice as many initial sounds. He is also more advanced at medial and final sounds, but not as much so. Regarding syllables, R is much better at using closed syllables, as evidenced by the number of CVC forms and the high proportion of closed syllables, 0.71, as contrasted with Jennika's 0.43. In terms of their ability to use multisyllabic phonetic forms, however, the two are the same. Their Proportions of Monosyllables are nearly identical, 0.57 and 0.59 for Jennika and R, respectively.

CONSONANT INVENTORY SHEET
Phonetic Forms   Child's name and age R 3;11

✓ initial   _____ medial   _____ final

mʊ	mɪt	mami		(nam)"	næna			
		mama		num	næno			
				(næn)				
				((nan))				
				naok				
bi	bʌk	{bebi}	daʊ	dɔk	(dʌdo)			gak gaga
bo	bʌʃ	(bebe)	do	daɪt	dæegi			gʌk gago
		bʌfpʌt	da	doʊ	dado			
		babo						
po	(paʧ)	(peo)	taɪ	tʌt	tʌtʌt			kom kitat
pɔɪ	pak	pʌsa	ti	(tap)"	tato			kak
paɪ		peto	to	taɪt	tʌbo			{kin}
		pafo		tʌf	tebo			(kɪn)
		pɛsɪf		(taʧ)"	tejo			
					tʌpo			
			taʊ ⌣ tajo					
	fef			(sʌk)"	sʌkʌ			
				sæs	{sɔrsi}			
				sɪt	{sʌsi}			
				sek	sigo			
				sup ⌣ suwa				
	wʌn	weo						(ŋa)" hat hæpo
	wop							haɪ hæos hanan
	wak							hɔrsi
	wɛp							heo
	wɪʃ							
				lam				

CONSONANT INVENTORY SHEET

Phonetic Forms   Child's name and age R 3; 11

_____ initial   ✓ medial   _____ final

		mami mama			nænʌ hanan næno				
		hæpo tʌpo			tʌtʌt kitat tato peto				sʌkə
		{bebi} {bebe} babo tʌbo tebo			(dʌdo)'''' dado				dægi gaga sigo gago
		pafo			pʌsə sʌsi pɛsɪf				
		suwə						tejo tajo	
		bʌfpʌt			{hɔrsi} {sɔrsi}				

Appendix C.4

CONSONANT INVENTORY SHEET
Phonetic Forms

Child's name and age __R 3;11__

____ initial   ____ medial   ✓ final

nʊm		(nan)				kɪŋ	
kom		kin					
lam		(næn)					
		(nan)					
(tap)		tʌt	bʌfpʌt	wɪtʃ		bʌk	
wop		(paf)	tʌtʌt			(sʌk)	
sʊp		hat	kitat			(kak)	
wɛp		(taɪt)				(dɔk)	
		(daɪt)				(gak)	
		mit				gʌk	
		sit				pak	
		(taf)"				naɔk	
						wak	
						sek	
fef	pɛsɪf	sæs		bʌʃ			
tʌf		haʊs					
dov							

CHILD SYLLABLE SHEET

Child's name and age ___ R 3;11 ___

Monosyllables / Multi-syllables

	CV	CVC	CVC$_2^n$	Comp. Red	Part. Red	Non-Red	Other Red	CVCVC	Other multi-syll.	Total
m	1	1		1	1					4
n		4			2					6
p	3	2				3		1	1	10
t	4	5			1	5		1		16
k		4						1		5
b	2	2		1	2				1	8
d	3	3			2	1				9
g		2		1	1					4
tʃ										
dʒ										
f		1								1
θ										
s		5			2	2			1	10
ʃ										
v										
ð							`			
z										
h	2	2				1		1	2	8
w		5							1	6
r										
l		1								1
j										
other segments										

C$_2^n$VC$_0^n$ (clusters c l u s t e r s)

Totals

	CV	CVC	CVC$_2^n$	C$_2^n$VC$_0^n$	Comp.R	Part.R	Non Red	Other Red	CVCVC	Other multi	Total
Total:	15	37			3	11	12		4	6	88
Vowel											
	V	VC	VC$_2^n$		VCV	VCV					

ITEM AND REPLICA SHEET

Child's name and age ___ R 3;11 ___

Child's Phonetic Inventory

Word initial segments

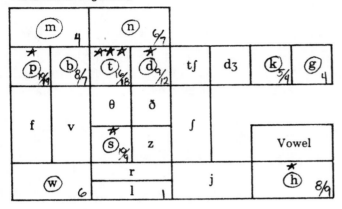

ⓜ 4		ⓝ 6/7					
★ ⓟ 14/14	ⓑ 8/7	★★★ ⓣ 16/18	★ ⓓ 9/12	tʃ	dʒ	ⓚ 5/4	ⓖ 4
f	v	θ	ð	ʃ		Vowel	
		★ ⓢ 10/9	z				
ⓦ 6		r		j		★ ⓗ 8/9	
		l 1					

Word medial consonants

(m) 2		(n) 3		rs 2/1		ŋ	
(p) 2	ⓑ 5/4	ⓣ 4	ⓓ 2/5	tʃ	dʒ	k 1	ⓖ 4
f	v	θ	ð	ʃ	3		
		(s) 3	z				
w 1		r		(j) 2		h	
		l					

Word final consonants

(m) 3		ⓝ 5/6				ŋ 1	
ⓟ 4	b	★ ⓣ 11/19	d	tʃ	dʒ	★ ⓚ 10/9	g
(f) 3	v	θ	ð	ʃ	3		
		(s) 2	z	1			
		r		ɾ			
		l		ɭ			

Child's Substitutions

Syllable initial consonants

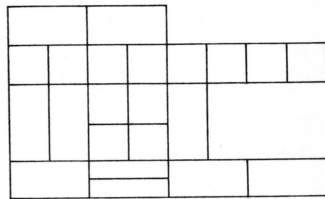

Ambisyllabic consonants

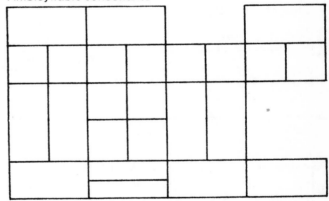

Syllable final consonants

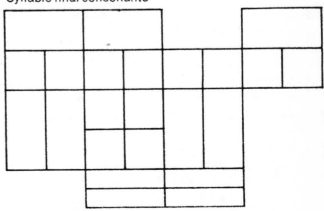

SUMMARY SHEET

Child's name and age ___R   3;11___

Sample size   lexical types: __90__   phonetic types: __101__   phonetic tokens: __105__   phonetic forms: __88__

Phonetic Analysis   Articulation Score __52__

Total Number of Sounds __18 (9)__   Criterion of Frequency _____4_____   ($\frac{178}{2} = \frac{89}{25}$)

word initial ___11___   word medial __3 (6)__   word final __4 (3)__

$$p\star^{m}\ b\ \ t\ ^{n}d\star\ k\ g \qquad (p)^{(m)}\ b\ \ t^{(n)}(d)\ g \qquad ^{(m)}\ n$$
$$w \qquad s\star \ \ h\star \qquad\qquad (s) \qquad (j) \qquad\qquad p\ \ t\star\ \ k\star$$
$$\qquad\qquad\qquad\qquad\qquad\qquad\qquad\qquad\qquad (f)\ \ (s)$$

syllable types: most frequent: CV (15)   CVC (37)   Proportion of: _____   Monosyllables _____   Closed syllables

Analysis of Homonymy

Ratio of Homonymous forms _____ :1   Homonymous types _____ :1

Proportion of Homonymous forms _____   Homonymous types _____

Substitution Analysis

	m	n	ŋ	p	b	t	d	k	g	tʃ	dʒ	f	θ	s	ʃ	v	ð	z	ʒ	w	j	r	l	h		
I			▨																▨							
A																										
F																				▨	▨			▨		

Proportion of Data _____ (/67) and Matches _____ (/) Acquired sounds _____

Phonological Process Analysis

Number of: _____ Processes _____ Affected Segments

FINAL CONSONANT DELETION

REDUCTION OF CONSONANT CLUSTERS

SYLLABLE DELETION AND REDUPLICATION

FRONTING OF PALATALS AND VELARS

STOPPING OF FRICATIVES AND AFFRICATES

SIMPLIFICATION OF LIQUIDS AND NASALS

OTHER PROCESSES

0.0–0.20   0.21–0.49   0.50–0.79   0.80–.100

APPENDIX D

Analysis of Homonymy for R 3;11

D.1. DISCUSSION OF THE ANALYSIS

After the phonetic analysis of R, 3;11, done in Chapter 3, the following lexical types should have phonetic types circled (in red) as homonymous: "arm," "bear," "belt," "boat," "butter," "cup," "desk," "feet," "fire," "flower," "foot," "hand," "man," "pear," "spider," "stick," "tent," "top (2)," "water," "window." In Step 1, these are entered onto a Homonymy Sheet. The result of this is shown in Appendix D.2. Note that "top" is circled because it has more than one homonymous form and should only be counted once (c.f., Step 1, 4.). Steps 2 and 3 involve the calculations of Ratios and Proportions of Homonymous Forms and Types. These can be seen on C.2 also. Then, the Ratios and Proportions can be entered onto the Summary Sheet. (Appendix C.7 can be used for this purpose.)

When R's Proportions are compared to Jennika, Joan, and W, we can see that he is closest to Joan, although his degree of homonymy is not as extensive. Section 7.1.2 discusses this issue in more detail. Generally, his use of homonymy is high but not extreme.

HOMONYMY SHEET

Child's name and age R 3;11

Homonymous forms	Homonymous types	No. of types
1. [nan]	arm, hand, man	3
2. [peo]	bear, pear	2
3. [tap]	belt, boat	2
4. [dʌdo]	butter, spider, water, window	4
5. [pat]	cup, feet, foot (top)	3
6. [sʌk]	desk, stick	2
7. [ha]	fire, flower	2
8. [tat]	tent, top	2
9. [ ]		
10. [ ]		
11. [ ]		
12. [ ]		
13. [ ]		
14. [ ]		
15. [ ]		

Summary of data

___8___ total number of homonymous forms (A)

__88__ total number of phonetic forms (B)

__80__ total number of nonhomonymous forms (C)

___20___ number of homonymous types (D)

___90___ number of lexical types (E)

___70___ number of nonhomonymous types (F)

Calculation of Extent of Homonymy

1. Ratio of Homonymous forms
   C:A __8__ : __80__ __10__ :1

2. Ratio of Homonymous types
   F:D __70__ : __20__ __4__ :1

3. Proportion of Homonymous forms
   0.09

4. Proportion of Homonymous types
   0.22

APPENDIX *E*

Substitution Analysis for R 3;11

E.1. DISCUSSION OF THE ANALYSIS

Step 1

Place a syllable boundary in "ba/nana." The next step applies to "bath/tub," "fire/man," "kitty/cat," "sea/gull," "tele/phone." Other consonants between vowels are ambisyllabic.

Step 2

Next, the words with similar target sounds are entered onto Consonant Inventory Sheets. Appendices E.3, E.4, and E.5 show these for syllable initial, intervocalic, and final sounds, respectively. If the target sounds are correct, only their utterance numbers are entered, with the last entry circled if they exceed five.

Step 3

The substitutes are then entered (in red) over their target sounds. Note that if a substitute is used in more than one phonetic type for a particular lexical type (e.g., "horsie" [sɔrsi] [sʌsi]) it is only entered once over the item, for example, "horsie" on Appendix E.3.

Step 4

In this step, we enter those substitutes that occur with *at least two* lexical types of a particular target sound onto the right side of the Item and Replica Sheet (c.f., Appendix E.2). If a target sound shows all matches, or else no substitute that occurs more than once, for example /p-/, then it is checked on the Item and Replica Sheet. Deletions are entered and counted as any other substitute.

Step 5

Here, the data are summarized onto the Summary Sheet (Appendix E.1) from the Item and Replica Sheet. Matches are shown with a check mark and substitutes (the two most frequent if more than one) are entered and circled.

Step 6

Last, we calculate the Proportion of Matches by determining the number of times the child matches without a substitution for an adult sound. For R, this turns out to be 0.23, a rather low proportion. Notice that it is even lower than Jennika's, 0.28, even though R has several sounds at his disposal. This is not very significant, however, because R has attempted several more sounds. Nonetheless, as is discussed in Chapter 7, language-delayed children tend to show lower Proportions of Matches. No sounds are checked in all possible positions so a zero is entered for Acquired Sounds. The Proportion of Data is calculated to be 0.46, a reasonable proportion for a spontaneous sample.

SUMMARY SHEET

Child's name and age ___R 3;11___

Sample size   **lexical types:** _____   **phonetic types:** _____   **phonetic tokens:** _____   **phonetic forms:** _____

Phonetic Analysis   Articulation Score _____

Total Number of Sounds _____   Criterion of Frequency _____   ($\overline{2} = \overline{25}$)

word initial _____   word medial _____   word final _____

syllable types: _____   **most frequent:** _____   **Proportion of:** _____   Monosyllables _____   **Closed syllables**

Analysis of Homonymy

Ratio of Homonymous forms _____:1   Homonymous types _____:1

Proportion of Homonymous forms _____   Homonymous types _____

Substitution Analysis

	m	n	ŋ	p	b	t	d	k	g	tʃ	dʒ	f	θ	s	ʃ	v	ð	z	ʒ	w	j	r	l	h	
I	ⓝ	—	▨	✓	ⓣp	ⓓ	ⓖs	ⓓ	—	—	—	ⓟh	—	ⓞ	—	—	—	—	▨	ⓟd	—	ⓦ	ⓣd	ⓗ	0.08 (1/2)
A	ⓝ	ⓞ	—	✓	ⓓʒ	✓	ⓖ	—	—	—	—	—	—	✓	—	—	—	—	—	—	—	—	—	—	0.38 (3/8)
F	✓	ⓞ	—	ⓣ	ⓟ	ⓟ	ⓞt	✓	—	—	—	ⓕ	✓	—	—	—	—	—	—	▨	ⓞʒ	ⓞʒ	▨	▨	0.30 (3/11)

Proportion of Data __0.46__ (31/67) and Matches __0.23__ (7/31) Acquired sounds __0__

Phonological Process Analysis

Number of:_____ Processes_____ Affected Segments

FINAL CONSONANT DELETION

REDUCTION OF CONSONANT CLUSTERS

SYLLABLE DELETION AND REDUPLICATION

FRONTING OF PALATALS AND VELARS

STOPPING OF FRICATIVES AND AFFRICATES

SIMPLIFICATION OF LIQUIDS AND NASALS

OTHER PROCESSES

0.0–0.20   0.21–0.49   0.50–0.79   0.80–.100

ITEM AND REPLICA SHEET

Child's name and age ____R 3; 11____

Child's Phonetic Inventory

Word initial segments

m		n					
p	b	t	d	tʃ	dʒ	k	g
f	v	θ	ð	ʃ			
		s	z			Vowel	
w		r		j		h	
		l					

Word medial consonants

m		n					ŋ
p	b	t	d	tʃ	dʒ	k	g
f	v	θ	ð	ʃ	ʒ		
		s	z				
w		r		j		h	
		l					

Word final consonants

m		n					ŋ
p	b	t	d	tʃ	dʒ	k	g
f	v	θ	ð	ʃ	ʒ		
		s	z				
		r		ɾ			
		l		l̩			

Child's Substitutions

Syllable initial consonants

n (2)		—					
✓	t (3) / p (3)	d (2)	g (3) / s (2)	—	—	d (2)	—
p (5) / h (2)	—	— / ∅(3)	— / —	—			
p (2) / d (2)		w(2) ∅(5) / t(2) d(2)		—		n (2)	

Ambisyllabic consonants

n (2)		∅ (2)					
—	✓	d(2) / ∅(2)	✓	—	—	g(2)	—
—	—	—	—	—	—		
		✓	—				
—		∅ (2) / —		—		—	

Syllable final consonants

✓		∅ (4)				—	
t(2)	p(2)	p(2)	∅(3) / t(2)	—	—	✓	—
—	—	f(2) / ✓	— / —	—	—		
		o(2) ∅(3) / o(4) ∅(4)	o(8) / o(4/5)				

CONSONANT INVENTORY SHEET

Lexical Types   Child's name and age R 3;11

✓ initial   ____ ambisyllabic   ____ final

b			d			dʒ			g		
3	ᵖball	b̄anana	25	ˢdesk	ᵍdoctor				63		
7	ᵖbear	ˢbasket	26	ᵏdog							
10	ᵗbed	ᵖboy		ˢdress							
12	ᵗbelt	ⁿbroom		ᵗdrum							
14	ᵗboat	ᵈbutter		ᵍduck							

p			t			tʃ			k		
57		ᵈspider	73	ᵈstove	ᵍtractor				20	ᵈcow	ᵈcandy
58			74	ᵈstar	bath/tub				44	ᵖcup	kitty/cat
59			75	ᵠstick					45		
			76	ᵖtop							
			(77)								

v			z			ʒ			ð		

f			s			ʃ			θ		
	ᵖfeet		63	ᶠsafe	ᵠspider		ˢshoe	ᵗshovel			
	ʰfire		64	ᵗslide							
	ᵖfish	ⁿflower	68	ᵠstar							
	ᵖfoot	tele/phone	71	ᵠstove							
	ᵖfork										

w			l			r			h		
56	ʰwheel	ᵖwaffle		ᵗᵈlight	ᵈladder		broom	tractor	40	ⁿhand	ⁿhammer
85		ᵈwater		ᵠslide	ᵗletter		brush	ʷrock	41		ˢhorsie
86		ᵖwhistle					dress		42		
90		ᵈwindow					ᵠdrum		43		
							r̆obe				

									vowel	ʰarm	ʰapple
											ᵗelephant

m			n						ŋ		
51	ⁿman		5	ᵖshake							
53	ⁿmilk	ᵇmarble									
54											
55											

CONSONANT INVENTORY SHEET

Lexical Types   Child's name and age R   3;11

_____ initial   ✓ ambisyllabic   _____ final

b 3			d 46	candy	dʒ			g		
50			69							
73			89							
p 1		paper	t	butter doctor tractor water kittycat	tʃ			k 6	doctor tractor	
v		shovel	z		ʒ			ð		
f 83		elephant	s 42	basket	ʃ			θ		
			88							
w		flower	l	elephant telephone	r 42		horsie marble	h		
								vowel		
m 53		hammer	n 5	candy				ŋ		
54		fireman		window						

CONSONANT INVENTORY SHEET

Lexical Types   Child's name and age R 3;11

_____ initial   _____ ambisyllabic   ✓ final

b	robe[p] bathtub[t] web[b]	d	bed[t] bird[d] hand[Ø] seed[t] slide[Ø]	dʒ		g	dog[k]
p	cup[t] top[t]	t	30 belt[Ø] boat[t] 36 40 (45)	basket[Ø]	tʃ 90		k	14 23 29 37 (52)
v 72		z			ʒ		ð	
f 62		s	27 desk[Ø] 43		ʃ 17	fish[v]	θ	bath[f]tub teeth[f]
w		l	ball[Ø] belf[f] tail[o] whale[Ø] wheel taweł[Ø,f] seagull[g]	apple[o] marble[o] shovel[o] table[o] waffle[Ø] whistle[Ø]	r	arm[Ø] bear[Ø] door[Ø] fire[Ø] pear[Ø] star[Ø]	ladder[o] butter[o] doctor[^] hammer[o] flower[—] letter[o] paper[o] spider[o] tractor[o] water[o]	h	vowel	shoe[p]
m 16 20 28	arm[n]	n	33 moon[Ø] 39 tent[Ø] 49 56	elephant[Ø] telephone[Ø]			ŋ 44	king[n]

APPENDIX F

Phonological Process Analysis for R 3;11

F.1. DISCUSSION OF THE ANALYSIS

Step 1. Initial sounds

The data from R are unusually difficult to analyze because there are several substitutions that are not often found. In fact, of the data from the 30 children analyzed in Ingram (1980), R's was the most difficult. It is included here, therefore, as a challenge test case for the procedures described. Also, it shows how many infrequent or idiosyncratic aspects of the child's data can be placed in perspective to the child's more pervasive processes. The first substitute on R's Summary Sheet (Practice Page 6.1) is [n] for /m-/. A check of Table 7 indicates process 22 or Apicalization. An examination of R's Consonant Inventory Sheets reveals that this process is the one that occurs. Also, a scan for other cases reveals that it also affects ambisyllabic /-m/. These are both entered on the Phonological Processes Sheet (c.f., Appendix F.3). The next, and most challenging substitutions are [t] [p] for /b-/, which require a look at the Lexicon Sheet. For [t], our first impression might be to consider it another case of Apicalization, that is, a preference for the alveolar over the labial position. The items this change occurs in, however, are [tap] "belt," "boat," and [tʌt] "bed." In the first two cases, it seems that Methathesis, that is, the changing of position by two segments, is actually what has happened. This also would account for the [p] substitute for /-t/. Because this

is neither a substitution or an assimilation, it is entered later, separately, on the Phonological Processes Sheet as an unnumbered process, occurring in adult words of the form /bVt/. The [t] in "bed," on the other hand, is the result of Assimilation or possibly Apicalization. The only evidence to help decide this is that /m-/ goes to [n] in both "man" [nan] and "milk" [naɑk], the latter form suggesting Apicalization. Here, we tentatively propose a process of Apicalization for /m-/, but do not claim it for /b-/ because only one form undergoes it. Recall that processes are only given for substitutes that occur at least twice for a single adult sound. The next initial sound with a substitute in Table 7 is /t-/, replaced with [d]. A check of the lexical types for R in Appendix E.3 confirms that this is a case of Voicing. Next, we can look for other cases of the process, which turns out also to affect /-t-/, /k-/, and /-k-/. The cases for /t-/, however, only involve "stove" and "star," words in which unaspirated [t]'s occur. In these cases, then, we consider the lax [d] as a correct production because English speakers hear unaspirated stops as voiced. The other instances of voicing can be entered as process 26 on the Phonological Processes Sheet (c.f., Appendix F.3). Contrary to this process, we then observe [p] for /b-/, or the use of Devoicing, a process that may be more characteristic of deviant speech. One case of Fronting occurs, that of [d] for /k-/, which also shows Voicing at work. Next, /d-/ goes to [g], the result of Velar Assimilation. This is entered under 24. For /f-/, we have Stopping to [p], but note that this only occurs in some of the examples. Otherwise, [h] occurs for /f-/. Other processes that can be found for initial substitutes in Table 7 are Cluster Reduction for /s-/ /r-/, and Gliding of /r-/.

The next substitute to examine is a peculiar one, [s] for /d-/. This occurs in "dress" [sæs] and "desk" [sʌk]. Also, a glance at other data shows "basket" [sʌkʌ]. The last two words suggest another metathesis rule, while "dress" would undergo assimilation. Because neither rule affects two cases under one adult sound, neither is entered on the Phonological Processes Sheet. The initial substitutes that are left are accounted for in the following ways: /h-/ goes to [n] due to Nasal Assimilation; /w/ to [p] as Glide Stopping, with further Glide Assimilation to [d] when a following [d] occurs, for example, "window" [dʌdo]; "water" [dʌdo] (assuming a voiced tap in "water"); Liquid Stopping for /l-/ to [d], with variable Devoicing to [t].

The processes that account for intervocalic and final substitutes are more typical of children at this level of development. Intervocalically, there are deletions of /-n-/, /-t-/, and [-r-] that can all be assigned to Cluster Reduction of /-nd-/, /-kt-/, and /-rC-/ clusters, respectively. The first cluster is already shown as 2 on the Phonological Processes Sheet, but /-kt-/ and /-rC-/ need to be added. For final segments, there is also Cluster Reduction for /-nt/ due to deletion of /n/ twice. Finally, there is Final Consonant Deletion of /-n/, /-d/, and /-r/, so that the nasals, liquids, and voiced stops are circled on the Phonological Processes Sheet. Vocalization occurs for /-l/ and /-r/, and this process is indicated as process 18.

The final voiced stops /-b/ and /-d/ both show Final Consonant Devoicing. The voiceless stops /-p/ and /-t/ show evidence for Metathesis. Recall that our first Metathesis rule accounts for the [p] for /-t/. For /-p/, however, there are "cup" [pat] and "top" [pat] which suggest that while R moves [p] to the end of a word when it occurs before /t/, he moves /-p/ to initial position if /t-/ or /k-/ occurs. A last, isolated change is the Labialization of /-θ/ to [f].

Last, we can look to see if any of the syllable processes operate. Following Step 1,4, we first observe Appendix E.4 to see if any dashes appear. None do, so we conclude that Reduction of Disyllables does not occur. There is one word with an unstressed pretonic syllable that is deleted, "banana," and three with internal unstressed syllables dropped—"elephant," "kittycat," and "telephone." We therefore circle Unstressed Syllable Deletion. Last, R's Syllable Sheet (Appendix C.5) indicates that Reduplications exist, so this process is circled.

The result of Step 1 is the establishment of several phonological processes for R 3;11. As stated earlier, R's data show an unusually high number of these.

Step 2

In this step, we decide whether or not to do a complete analysis. For the purpose of demonstration, we will do a partial one.

Step 3

Here, we go back to the Consonant Inventory Sheets—Lexical Types and calculate the proportions for the number of lexical types that meet the conditions for each process and actually undergo it. These are given in Appendix F.3. The actual lexical types that either undergo or do not undergo each process are shown in Appendix F.2. Note the following aspects of these entries: 1) only lexical types are entered when the adult sound shows at least two cases of the process; 2) Final Consonant Deletion only refers to single consonants; clusters are considered under Cluster Reduction; 3) when not all members of a class show Final Consonant Deletion, the members that do are shown on the Phonological Processes Sheet.

Step 4

In this last step, we transfer the proportions for each process onto the Summary Sheet (c.f., Appendix F.4). Note that because of space limitations, the "Other" processes part of the Sheet has been altered so that all processes may be entered. Also, note that processes only are put on the Summary Sheet if they meet the Criterion of Frequency, which in R's case is 4. This eliminates many of the infrequent processes on the Phonological Processes Sheet.

Appendix F.2 LEXICAL TYPES IN R 3;11 THAT DO AND DO NOT UNDERGO THE PHONOLOGICAL PROCESSES CIRCLED ON THE PHONOLOGICAL PROCESSES SHEET

		Lexical Types	
Process		Undergo Process	Do Not Undergo Process
Deletion of Final Consonants			
(1) nasals	/-n/	moon, telephone	fireman, man, one
liquids	/-r/	door, fire, star	bear, pear
	/-l/	ball, towel	tail, whale, wheel, towel
(2) voiced stops	/-d/	bird, slide	bed, seed
Reduction in Consonant Clusters			
(6)	C/r-/	broom, brush, dress, drum, tractor	
(8)	/s/C-	star, stove, spider slide, stick, snake	
	/-nd-/	candy, window	
	/-nt/	tent, elephant	
	/-rC-/	horsie, marble	horsie
	/-kt-/	tractor, doctor	
(13) Fronting of velars	/k-/	cow, candy, kittycat	kittycat, comb, king
(14) Initial stopping	/f-/	feet, fish, foot, fork, tele/phone	fire, flower
(17) Gliding	/r-/	robe, rock	
(18) Vocalization	/-r/	bear, pear	door, fire, star
	/-l/	tail, whale, wheel, towel	ball, towel
	/-l̩/	(six cases)	whistle
	/-ɾ/	(nine cases)	
(26) Voicing	/-t-/	butter, water	
	/k-/	cow, candy	cup, kittycat, comb, king
	/-k-/	doctor, tractor	basket
(22) Apicalization	/m-/	man, milk	marble, meat, mommy, mama, moon
	/-m-/	hammer, fireman	mama, mommy
Glide Stopping	/w-/	waffle, water, whistle, window	wheel, one, web, whale, witch
Initial Devoicing	/b-/	ball, bear, bed, boy	butter, baby, bathtub, bee, bird, book, brush, broom
	/l-/	letter, light	letter, light
Liquid Stopping	/l-/	light(2x), ladder, letter	
(27) Final Devoicing	/-b/	web, robe, bathtub	
	/-d/	bed, seed	
(23) Labialization	/-θ/	bath, tub, teeth	
(24) Velar Assimilation			
	/d-/	dog(2x), duck, doctor	dog, desk
Nasal Assimilation			
	/h-/	hand, hammer	
Glide Assimilation			
	/w-/	water, window	
Metathesis		belt, boat top, cup	

PHONOLOGICAL PROCESSES SHEET

Child's name and age R   3;11

Syllable Structure Processes

Deletion of Final Consonants (FCD):

(1) nasals: /-m/   /-n/ (0.40 (3/5))   /-ŋ/

(3) voiceless stops: /-p/   /-t/   /-k/

(2) voiced stops: /-b/   /-d/ (0.50 (3/4))   /-g/

(4) voiced fricatives: /-v/   /-ð/   /-ʒ/   /-dʒ/

(5) voiceless fricatives: /-f/   /-θ/   /-s/   /-ʃ/   /-tʃ/

other: /-l/ (0.30 (3/6))   /-r/ (0.60 (3/5))

Reduction of Consonant Clusters (CR):

	(6) Liquids		(7) Nasals		(8) /s/ clusters
	C/l/-	C/r/-	-NCvd	-NCvless	/s/C-
reduced to C		1.00 (5/5)		1.00 (2/2)	0.50 (3/6)
C deleted					0.50 (3/6)
cluster deleted					
Total		1.00 (5/5)		1.00 (2/2)	1.00 (6/6)

Other Processes: /-k+-/→/-k-/ 1.00 (2/2)   /-rc-/→/-c-/ 0.67 (2/3)   /-nd-/→/-d-/ 1.00 (2/2)

Syllable Deletion

(9)   Reduction of Disyllables (RD) _____

(10)   Unstressed syllable deletion USD) 1.00 (4/4)

(11)   Reduplication 0.50 (13/26)

Substitution Processes

Fronting

syllable position	(12) of Palatals (PF)				(13) of Velars (VF)		
	/ʃ/	/ʒ/	/tʃ/	/dʒ/	/k/	/g/	/ŋ/
initial					0.50 (3/6)		
intervocalic							
final							

Stopping (S)

(14) of Initial Voiceless Fricatives				(15) of Initial Voiced Fricatives			
/f/	/θ/	/s/	/ʃ/	/v/	/ð/	/z/	/ʒ/
0.67 (5/7)							

(16)   of Affricates

/tʃ/	/dʒ/

SUMMARY SHEET

Child's name and age ___R 3;11___

| Sample size | lexical types: _____ | phonetic types: _____ | phonetic tokens: _____ | phonetic forms: _____ |

Phonetic Analysis Articulation Score _____

Total Number of Sounds _____ Criterion of Frequency _____ ($\overline{2} = \overline{25}$)

word initial _____ word medial _____ word final _____

| syllable types: | most frequent: _____ | Proportion of: _____ | Monosyllables _____ | Closed syllables |

Analysis of Homonymy

Ratio of Homonymous forms ____:1 Homonymous types ____:1

Proportion of Homonymous forms _____ Homonymous types _____

Substitution Analysis

	m	n	ŋ	p	b	t	d	k	g	tʃ	dʒ	f	θ	s	ʃ	v	ð	z	ʒ	w	j	r	l	h	
I			▨																▨						
A																									
F																				▨	▨			▨	

Proportion of Data _____ (/67) and Matches _____ (/) Acquired sounds _____

Phonological Process Analysis

Number of: __8__ Processes __7__ Affected Segments

FINAL CONSONANT DELETION

REDUCTION OF CONSONANT CLUSTERS

			(6) c /r/-
			(8) /s/ c-

SYLLABLE DELETION AND REDUPLICATION

		(11) Red.	(10) USD

FRONTING OF PALATALS AND VELARS

STOPPING OF FRICATIVES AND AFFRICATES

		(14) /f-/	

SIMPLIFICATION OF LIQUIDS AND NASALS

		/-l/	(18) /l, r/

OTHER PROCESSES

	Devoicing /b-/	(21) Velar assim /d-/	(27) Devoicing /-b, -d/
	Glide Stopping /w-/		Metathesis
			Liquid Stopping /l-/

| 0.0–0.20 | 0.21–0.49 | 0.50–0.79 | 0.80–.100 |

Simplification of Liquids and Nasals

(17) Liquid Gliding (LG))

	substitutes					substitutes			
/r-/	[w]	1.00 (2/2)	[j]	_____	/-r-/	[w]	_____	[j]	_____
/l-/	[w]	_____	[j]	_____	/-l-/	[w]	_____	[j]	_____

(18) Vocalization (V):

/ɹ/	[ ]	1.00 (9/9)	[ ]	_____	/-r/	[o]	0.40 (2/5)	[ ]	_____
/l/	[ ]	0.86 (6/7)	[ ]	_____	/-l/	[o]	0.67 (4/6)	[ ]	_____

(19) Denasalization (DN):

	initial	intervocalic	final	total
/m/	_____		_____	_____
/n/	_____		_____	_____
/ŋ/		_____	_____	_____

Other Substitution Processes

Process	Target	Change	Syllable position	
(22) Apicalization	/ m /	[n]	initial	0.29 (2/7)
	/ /	[ ]	ambisyllabic	0.50 (2/4)
(23) Labialization	/ θ /	[f]	final	1.00 (2/2)
Liquid stopping	/ e /	[t,d]	initial	1.00 (4/4)
Glide stopping	/ w /	[p,d]	initial	0.44 (4/9)
	/ /	[ ]	_____	
Metathesis	/ /	[ ]	/bʌt/ → tʌp	1.00 (2/2)
	/ /	[ ]	/t,kʌp/ → [pʌt,k]	1.00 (2/2)

Assimilation Processes

Process	Sounds	Change	Environment	
(24) Velar assim.	/ d /	[g,k]	regressive	0.67 (4/6)
(26) Voicing	/ t /	[d]	ambisyllabic	1.00 (2/2)
"	/ k /	[g]	ambisyllabic	0.67 (2/3)
"	/ /	[d]	initial	0.29 (2/7)
(27) Final devoicing	/ b /	[p,t]	final	1.00 (3/3)
	/ d /	[t]	final	1.00 (2/2)
Initial devoicing	/ b /	[p,t]	initial	0.33 (4/12)
Nasal assim.	/ h /	[n]	initial	1.00 (2/2)
Glide assim.	/ w /	[d]	initial	1.00 (2/2)

APPENDIX G

Complete Analysis
for Jennika 1;5

SUMMARY SHEET

Child's name and age ___Jennika 1;5___

Sample size	lexical types: _42_	phonetic types: _73_	phonetic tokens: _90_	phonetic forms: _70_

Phonetic Analysis Articulation Score _.31_

Total Number of Sounds _12_   Criterion of Frequency ___2___   ($\frac{112}{2} = \frac{56}{25}$)

word initial _5_   word medial _4_   word final _3_

```
    m                                                      m*
    p      b***  d***          p    b    t*   d**              t**
    w*                                                             ts
```

syllable types:	most frequent:	CV (17) CVC (13) CVCV (13)	Proportion of: _0.57_	Monosyllables _0.43_	Closed syllables

Analysis of Homonymy

Ratio of Homonymous forms _22_ :1   Homonymous types _6_ :1

Proportion of Homonymous forms _0.04_   Homonymous types _0.14_

Substitution Analysis

	m	n	ŋ	p	b	t	d	k	g	tʃ	dʒ	f	θ	s	ʃ	v	ð	z	ʒ	w	j	r	l	h	
I	✓		▨	✓	✓		✓	ⓓ						Ø						✓		ⓦ		Ø	0.56(5/9)
A								✝																	0.00(%)
F		ⓜ				Ø	Ø	ⓣ+					✝	Ø						▨		Ø		▨	0.00(%)

Proportion of Data _0.25_ (17/67) and Matches _0.29_ (5/17) Acquired sounds _0_

Phonological Process Analysis

Number of: _9_ Processes _10_ Affected Segments

FINAL CONSONANT DELETION

				(2) /-d/
	(3)/-k/	(5) /-s/	(3) /-t/	

REDUCTION OF CONSONANT CLUSTERS

			(8) /s/ c-

SYLLABLE DELETION AND REDUPLICATION

(9) RD		(11) Reduplication	

FRONTING OF PALATALS AND VELARS

		(13)/k-/ /-k-/ /-k/	

STOPPING OF FRICATIVES AND AFFRICATES

			final /-θ/

SIMPLIFICATION OF LIQUIDS AND NASALS

			(17) /r-/

OTHER PROCESSES

			(23) /-n/
			(21) /h-/
			(26) /k-/
			Deletion of Liquids /-r/

0.0–0.20	0.21–0.49	0.50–0.79	0.80–.100

ITEM AND REPLICA SHEET

Child's name and age ___Jennika 1;5___

Child's Phonetic Inventory

Word initial segments

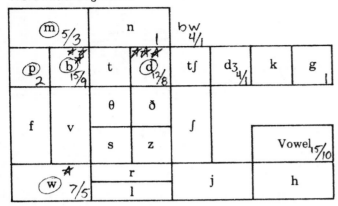

Child's Substitutions

Syllable initial consonants

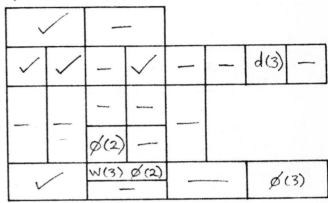

Word medial consonants

m		n					ŋ	
(p) 4/3	(b) 4/2	(t) 6/5	(d) 9/7	tʃ	dʒ	k 1	g 2/1	
f	v	θ	ð	ʃ	3			
		s	z					
w 2/1		r		j		h		
		l						

Ambisyllabic consonants

—	—			—
—	—	—	—	—	—	†(2)	—
—	—	—	—			
—	—	—	—			
—	—	—	—			

Word final consonants

(m) 5/4		n			ŋ	
p 2/1	b	(t) 2/1	d	(tʃ) 4/3	dʒ	k	g
							? 1
f	v	θ	ð	ʃ	3	
		s 1	z	ʃ 1		
		r		ɾ		
		l 1		ɫ		

Syllable final consonants

—	m(4)			—	
—	—	∅(3)	∅(2)	—	—	∅(3) †(2)	—
—	—	†(2)	—	—	—	
—	—	∅(2)	—			
		∅(2)				

PHONOLOGICAL PROCESSES SHEET

Child's name and age _Jennika 1;5_

Syllable Structure Processes

Deletion of Final Consonants (FCD):

(1) nasals: /-m/ _____ /-n/ _____ /-ŋ/ _____

(3) voiceless stops: /-p/ _____ /-t/ **0.60 (3/5)** /-k/ **0.43 (3/7)**

(2) voiced stops: /-b/ _____ /-d/ **1.00 (2/2)** /-g/ _____

(4) voiced fricatives: /-v/ _____ /-ð/ _____ /-z/ _____ /-dʒ/ _____

(5) voiceless fricatives: /-f/ _____ /-θ/ _____ /-s/ **0.40 (2/5)** /-ʃ/ _____ /-tʃ/ _____

liquids: /-r/ **1.00 (2/2)**

Reduction of Consonant Clusters (CR):

	(6) Liquids		(7) Nasals		(8) /s/ clusters
	C/l/-	C/r/-	-NCvd	-NCvless	/s/C-
reduced to C	_____	_____	_____	_____	**1.00 (2/2)**
C deleted	_____	_____	_____	_____	
cluster deleted	_____	_____	_____	_____	
Total	_____	_____	_____	_____	**1.00 (2/2)**

Syllable Deletion

(9) Reduction of Disyllables (RD) **0.15 (2/13)** _____

(11) Reduplication **0.79 (15/19)** _____

(10) Unstressed syllable deletion USD) _____

Substitution Processes

Fronting

(12) of Palatals (PF)

syllable position	/ʃ/	/ʒ/	/tʃ/	/dʒ/
initial	_____	_____	_____	_____
intervocalic	_____	_____	_____	_____
final	_____	_____	_____	_____

(13) of Velars (VF)

	/k/	/g/	/ŋ/
initial	**0.60 (3/5)**	_____	_____
intervocalic	**0.60 (3/5)**	_____	_____
final	**0.67 (2/3)**	_____	_____

Stopping (S)

(14) of Initial Voiceless Fricatives

/f/	/θ/	/s/	/ʃ/
_____	_____	_____	_____

(15) of Initial Voiced Fricatives

/v/	/ð/	/z/	/ʒ/
_____	_____	_____	_____

(16) of Affricates

/tʃ/	/dʒ/
_____	_____

Simplification of Liquids and Nasals

(17) Liquid Gliding (LG))

substitutes   substitutes

/r-/ [w] (1.00 (3/3)) [j] _____   /-r-/ [w] _____   [j] _____

/l-/ [w] _____   [j] _____   /-l-/ [w] _____   [j] _____

(18) Vocalization (V):

/ɼ/ [ ] _____   [ ] _____   [ ] _____   [ ] _____

/l̩/ [ ] _____   [ ] _____   [ ] _____   [ ] _____

(19) Denasalization (DN):

	initial	intervocalic	final	total
/m/	_____	_____	_____	_____
/n/	_____	_____	_____	_____
/ŋ/		_____	_____	_____

Other Substitution Processes

Process	Target	Change	Syllable position	
Stopping of Final Consonants	/ θ /	[t]	final	1.00 (2/2)
(23) Labialization	/ n /	[m]	final	0.80 (4/5)
(21) Deletion of initial consonants	/ /	[ ]	_____	
	/ h /	[∅]	initial	1.00 (3/3)
_____	/ /	[ ]	_____	_____
_____	/ /	[ ]	_____	_____
_____	/ /	[ ]	_____	_____
_____	/ /	[ ]	_____	_____

Assimilation Processes

Process	Sounds	Change	Environment	
(26) Prevocalic voicing	/ k /	[g,d]	initial	1.00 (5/5)
_____	/ /	[ ]	_____	_____
_____	/ /	[ ]	_____	_____
_____	/ /	[ ]	_____	_____
_____	/ /	[ ]	_____	_____
_____	/ /	[ ]	_____	_____
_____	/ /	[ ]	_____	_____
_____	/ /	[ ]	_____	_____

Appendix G.4

CONSONANT INVENTORY SHEET

Lexical Types Child's name and age Jennika 1,5

✓ initial ___ ambisyllabic ___ final

b: 3, 4, 5, 6, (7)	d: 1, 13, 14, 15	dʒ: 23	g: [d] get down
p: 31 poop, 38	t	tʃ: [d] chair	k: [d,g] cookie, [dʒ] ice cream, [d] kitty, [d] Kristen
v	z	ʒ	ð
f	s: 36, [ø] spoon, [ø] sweater	ʃ: 37	θ
w: 39, 41, 42	l: [w,ø] blanket	r: [w] ride, [w] rock, [ø] ice cream, [ø] Kristen, [w] ring rosy	h: 21, [ø] hat, [ø] hi, [ø] hot
			vowel: 1, 2, 16, 17, 30, [dʒ] ice cream
m: 26, 27, 28	n: 29		ŋ

CONSONANT INVENTORY SHEET

Lexical Types   Child's name and age _Jennika 1;5_

_____ initial   ✓ ambisyllabic   _____ final

b			d ₁₃			dʒ			g		
p ₂			t ₂₄		Kristen ᵈ / sweater ⁻ / water ʷ	tʃ			k 7		blanket ⁺ / cookie ⁺ᵍᵈⁱ
v			z		ring rosy ⁻	ʒ			ð		
f			s		Kristen ᵒ̸	ʃ			θ		
w			l			r			h		
									vowel	
m ₂₆			n						ŋ		blanket ᵒ̸

CONSONANT INVENTORY SHEET

Lexical Types   Child's name and age <u>Jennika 1;5</u>

_____ initial   _____ ambisyllabic   ✓ final

b	bib^ø		d	bird^ø ride^ø		dʒ			g	dog^v egg^ø
p 40	poop^v		t 20	hat^tS blanket^ø,t hot^v get^ø/down out^ø		tʃ			k	bike^ø book^ø,?,t box^tS rock^ø,v walk^t
v			z			ʒ			ð	
f			s 23	box^tS juice^ø,t		ʃ			θ	bath^t mouth^t
w			l	all/done	r	chair^ø more^ø		h	
			! 2	apple^u	r˞		sweater water^ʌ,a	vowel	
m	ice cream^ø	n 48	down^ø,m all done^m spoon^m					ŋ	ring, rosy

HOMONYMY SHEET

Child's name and age ___Jennika 1;5___

Homonymous forms	Homonymous types	No. of types
1. [bat]	bath, blanket	2
2. [aɪ]	eye, hi	2
3. [wa]	ring rosy, rock	2
4. [ ]		
5. [ ]		
6. [ ]		
7. [ ]		
8. [ ]		
9. [ ]		
10. [ ]		
11. [ ]		
12. [ ]		
13. [ ]		
14. [ ]		
15. [ ]		

Summary of data

___3___ total number of homonymous forms (A)

___70___ total number of phonetic forms (B)

___67___ total number of nonhomonymous forms (C)

___6___ number of homonymous types (D)

___42___ number of lexical types (E)

___36___ number of nonhomonymous types (F)

Calculation of Extent of Homonymy

1. Ratio of Homonymous forms
   C:A __67__ : __3__ __22__ :1

2. Ratio of Homonymous types
   F:D __36__ : __6__ __6__ :1

3. Proportion of Homonymous forms
   __0.04__

4. Proportion of Homonymous types
   __0.14__

CONSONANT INVENTORY SHEET

Phonetic Forms   Child's name and age _Jennika 1;5_

✓ initial
_____ medial
_____ final

{mɔ} {mæt} mami	nɔ						
{mo}							
{mʌ}							
bɪ bät	dɛ	{duti}	dʒu {dʒuʃ} dʒudʒu			gigi
baɪ {bat} bati	daʊ~dʌm {didi}	{dʒut}				
bi batʃi {babaɪ}	{dodi}					
{ba} {baʏ} {babaɪ}	{digi}					
{bʌ} {bʌt} {baʊ}	dæʊdi					
{bʌt} {bʌbʊ}	dɔdi					
	didʌm					
	dɪti					
	dɪdɪn					
pʌm pipi							
bwa {bwat {bwaki}			haɪ				
{bwati}						
waɪ {waʃ} {wati}			i {atʃ} {ædʌm}				
wä {watʃ} {wa}			aɪ {aɪtʃ} {ɔdʌm}				
{wawa}			aʊ {apʊ}				
{wʌwʌ}			{ap} {æpʊl}				
			{ʌpt} api				
	ʃu	{at} ati				
		atⁿ {aɪdi}				
		{aɪ}				

CONSONANT INVENTORY SHEET
Phonetic Forms   Child's name and age _Jennika 1;5_

_____ initial   ✓ medial   _____ final

		mami							

mami

{apʊ / æpɒl}
pipi
api

{bwati / bati}
dʊti
ati
dɪti
wati

bwaki

{babaɪ / bəbaɪ}
{bʌbɒ / bʌbʌ}

{ædʌm / ɔdʌm}
{didi / dodi}
dædi
dɔdi
didʌm
ɑɪdi
dɪdɪn

dʒudʒu

{digi / gigi}

{wʌwʌ / wawa}

CONSONANT INVENTORY SHEET
Phonetic Forms   Child's name and age Jennika 1;5

_____ initial   _____ medial   ✓ final

pʌm {ʔædʌm}			dɪdɪn				
dʌm (ɔdʌm)							
dɪdʌm							
{ap}		at"	b̈at		batʃ		baʔ
(ʌp)			(bat)⁺ bwat		{atʃ}		
			{bɒt} mæet		(aItʃ)		
			(bʌt)		watʃ		
			dʒʊt				
					waʃ		
			æppɒl				

CHILD SYLLABLE SHEET

Child's name and age **Jennika 1;5**

Monosyllables / Multi-syllables

	CV	CVC	CVC_2^n	Comp. Red	Part. Red	Non-Red	Other Red	CVCVC	Other multi-syll.	Total
m	3	1			1					5
n	1									1
p		1		1						2
t										
k										
b	5	5			4	1				15
d	2	1		1	4	2		2		12
g				1						1
tʃ										
dʒ	1	2								4
f										
θ										
s	1									1
ʃ	1									1
v										
ð										
z										
h	1									1
w	2	3		2		1				8
r										
l										
j										

other segments ___ ___ ___

clusters

	CV	$C_2^nVC_0^n$	Other multi-syll.	Total
bw		2	2	4

Summary

	CV	CVC	CVC_2^n	$C_2^nVC_0^n$	Comp.R	Part.R	Non Red	Other Red	CVCVC	Other multi	Total
Total:	17	13	0	2	6	9	4	0	2	2	70
Vowel	3	5	0			0	4			3	
	V	VC	VC_2^n		VCV	VCV					

LEXICON SHEET

Child's name and age _Jennika 1;5_

lexical	types phonetic	lexical	types phonetic	lexical	types phonetic	lexical	types phonetic
1. all done	¹ æd∧m (2x)	15. down	³¹ daʊ	35. rock	⁶¹ (wa)		
	² ɔd∧m		³² d∧m		⁶² wati		
2. apple	³ apʊ	16. egg	³³ i	36. see	⁶³ si (2x)		
	⁴ æpɒl	17. eye	³⁴ (aɪ)	37. shoe	⁶⁴ ʃu (2x)		
3. bath	⁵ (bat)	18. get down	³⁵ did∧m	38. spoon	⁶⁵ p∧m		
4. bib	⁶ bɪ	19. hat	³⁶ atʃ (2x)	39. sweater	⁶⁶ waʃ		
5. bike	⁷ baɪ		³⁷ aɪtʃ		⁶⁷ watʃ		
6. bird	⁸ bi	20. hot	³⁸ at	40. up	⁶⁸ ap (3x)		
7. blanket	⁹ bwa		³⁹ ati		⁶⁹ ∧p		
	¹⁰ (bat)	21. hi	⁴⁰ aɪdi		⁷⁰ api (2x)		
	¹¹ bwaki		⁴¹ (aɪ) (2x)	41. walk	⁷¹ at		
	¹² bwati (2x)		⁴² haɪ	42. water	⁷² wawa		
	¹³ bwat	22. ice cream	⁴³ dʒʊ dʒʊ		⁷³ w∧w∧		
	¹⁴ bati	23. juice	⁴⁴ dʒʊ (2x)				
8. book	¹⁵ ba (2x)		⁴⁵ dʒʊs (2x)				
	¹⁶ b∧ (2x)		⁴⁶ dʒʊt				
	¹⁷ ba?	24. kitty	⁴⁷ dɪti				
	¹⁸ bɒt (2x)	25. Kristen	⁴⁸ dɪdɪn				
	¹⁹ b∧t	26. mommy	⁴⁹ mami				
9. box	²⁰ batʃ	27. move	⁵⁰ mɔ				
10. bye bye	²¹ babaɪ		⁵¹ mo				
	²² bəbaɪ		⁵² m∧				
11. chair	²³ dɛ	28. mouth	⁵³ mɒt				
12. cookie	²⁴ duti (2x)	29. no	⁵⁴ no				
	²⁵ didi (2x)	30. out	⁵⁵ aʊ				
	²⁶ dodi	31. pee	⁵⁶ pipi				
	²⁷ digi	32. poop	⁵⁷ b∧bo				
	²⁸ gigi		⁵⁸ b∧bʊ				
13. daddy	²⁹ dædi	33. ride	⁵⁹ waɪ				
14. dog	³⁰ dɔdi	34. ring rosy	⁶⁰ (wa)				

Index

ANALYSIS FORMS
for
Procedures for the Phonological Analysis of Children's Language

To: UNIVERSITY PARK PRESS
300 North Charles Street
Baltimore, Maryland 21201

ORDER FORM

Please include full
payment or credit card
charge authorization
with this order.

Send me _____ set(s) of **Analysis Forms** for **Ingram: Procedures for the Phonological Analysis of Children's Language** (each set contains: 20 lexicon sheets, 30 consonant inventory sheets, 10 phonological processes sheets, 10 item and replica sheets, 10 child syllable sheets, 10 homonymy sheets) at **$9.95 per set.**

Amount enclosed in full payment of this order _____

Charge this purchase to my ☐ American Express ☐ Master Charge

☐ VISA   Card expiration date_____

Name _____

Address _____

Account No. _____

_____ Zip Code _____

Signature _____

Thank you

*Price subject to change without notice. Analysis forms are nonreturnable.

ANALYSIS FORMS
for
Procedures for the Phonological Analysis of Children's Language

To: UNIVERSITY PARK PRESS
300 North Charles Street
Baltimore, Maryland 21201

ORDER FORM

Please include full
payment or credit card
charge authorization
with this order.

Send me _____ set(s) of **Analysis Forms** for **Ingram: Procedures for the Phonological Analysis of Children's Language** (each set contains: 20 lexicon sheets, 30 consonant inventory sheets, 10 phonological processes sheets, 10 item and replica sheets, 10 child syllable sheets, 10 homonymy sheets) at **$9.95 per set.**

Amount enclosed in full payment of this order _____

Charge this purchase to my ☐ American Express ☐ Master Charge

☐ VISA   Card expiration date_____

Name _____

Address _____

Account No. _____

_____ Zip Code _____

Signature _____

Thank you

*Price subject to change without notice. Analysis forms are nonreturnable.

ANALYSIS FORMS
for
Procedures for the Phonological Analysis of Children's Language

To: UNIVERSITY PARK PRESS
300 North Charles Street
Baltimore, Maryland 21201

ORDER FORM

Please include full
payment or credit card
charge authorization
with this order.

Send me _____ set(s) of **Analysis Forms** for **Ingram: Procedures for the Phonological Analysis of Children's Language** (each set contains: 20 lexicon sheets, 30 consonant inventory sheets, 10 phonological processes sheets, 10 item and replica sheets, 10 child syllable sheets, 10 homonymy sheets) at **$9.95 per set.**

Amount enclosed in full payment of this order _____

Charge this purchase to my ☐ American Express ☐ Master Charge

☐ VISA   Card expiration date_____

Name _____

Address _____

Account No. _____

_____ Zip Code _____

Signature _____

Thank you

*Price subject to change without notice. Analysis forms are nonreturnable.

ANALYSIS FORMS
for
Procedures for the Phonological Analysis of Children's Language

To: UNIVERSITY PARK PRESS
300 North Charles Street
Baltimore, Maryland 21201

ORDER FORM

Please include full
payment or credit card
charge authorization
with this order.

Send me _____ set(s) of **Analysis Forms** for **Ingram: Procedures for the Phonological Analysis of Children's Language** (each set contains: 20 lexicon sheets, 30 consonant inventory sheets, 10 phonological processes sheets, 10 item and replica sheets, 10 child syllable sheets, 10 homonymy sheets) at **$9.95 per set.**

Amount enclosed in full payment of this order _____

Charge this purchase to my ☐ American Express ☐ Master Charge

☐ VISA   Card expiration date_____

Name _____

Address _____

Account No. _____

_____ Zip Code _____

Signature _____

Thank you

***Price subject to change without notice. Analysis forms are nonreturnable.**

ANALYSIS FORMS
for
Procedures for the Phonological Analysis of Children's Language

To: UNIVERSITY PARK PRESS
300 North Charles Street
Baltimore, Maryland 21201

ORDER FORM

Please include full
payment or credit card
charge authorization
with this order.

Send me _____ set(s) of **Analysis Forms** for **Ingram: Procedures for the Phonological Analysis of Children's Language** (each set contains: 20 lexicon sheets, 30 consonant inventory sheets, 10 phonological processes sheets, 10 item and replica sheets, 10 child syllable sheets, 10 homonymy sheets) at **$9.95 per set.**

Amount enclosed in full payment of this order _____

Charge this purchase to my ☐ American Express ☐ Master Charge

☐ VISA   Card expiration date_____

Name _____

Address _____

Account No. _____

_____ Zip Code _____

Signature _____

Thank you

***Price subject to change without notice. Analysis forms are nonreturnable.**

ANALYSIS FORMS
for
Procedures for the Phonological Analysis of Children's Language

To: UNIVERSITY PARK PRESS
300 North Charles Street
Baltimore, Maryland 21201

ORDER FORM

Please include full
payment or credit card
charge authorization
with this order.

Send me _____ set(s) of **Analysis Forms** for **Ingram: Procedures for the Phonological Analysis of Children's Language** (each set contains: 20 lexicon sheets, 30 consonant inventory sheets, 10 phonological processes sheets, 10 item and replica sheets, 10 child syllable sheets, 10 homonymy sheets) at **$9.95 per set.**

Amount enclosed in full payment of this order _____

Charge this purchase to my ☐ American Express ☐ Master Charge

☐ VISA   Card expiration date_____

Name _____

Address _____

Account No. _____

_____ Zip Code _____

Signature _____

Thank you

***Price subject to change without notice. Analysis forms are nonreturnable.**

ANALYSIS FORMS
for
Procedures for the Phonological Analysis of Children's Language

To: UNIVERSITY PARK PRESS
    300 North Charles Street
    Baltimore, Maryland 21201

ORDER FORM

Please include full
payment or credit card
charge authorization
with this order.

Send me _____ set(s) of **Analysis Forms** for **Ingram: Procedures for the Phonological Analysis of Children's Language** (each set contains: 20 lexicon sheets, 30 consonant inventory sheets, 10 phonological processes sheets, 10 item and replica sheets, 10 child syllable sheets, 10 homonymy sheets) at **$9.95 per set.**

Amount enclosed in full payment of this order _____

Charge this purchase to my ☐ American Express ☐ Master Charge

☐ VISA   Card expiration date_____

Name _____

Address _____

Account No. _____

_____ Zip Code _____

Signature _____

Thank you

Price subject to change without notice. Analysis forms are nonreturnable.

- -

ANALYSIS FORMS
for
Procedures for the Phonological Analysis of Children's Language

To: UNIVERSITY PARK PRESS
    300 North Charles Street
    Baltimore, Maryland 21201

ORDER FORM

Please include full
payment or credit card
charge authorization
with this order.

Send me _____ set(s) of **Analysis Forms** for **Ingram: Procedures for the Phonological Analysis of Children's Language** (each set contains: 20 lexicon sheets, 30 consonant inventory sheets, 10 phonological processes sheets, 10 item and replica sheets, 10 child syllable sheets, 10 homonymy sheets) at **$9.95 per set.**

Amount enclosed in full payment of this order _____

Charge this purchase to my ☐ American Express ☐ Master Charge

☐ VISA   Card expiration date_____

Name _____

Address _____

Account No. _____

_____ Zip Code _____

Signature _____

Thank you

Price subject to change without notice. Analysis forms are nonreturnable.

- -

ANALYSIS FORMS
for
Procedures for the Phonological Analysis of Children's Language

To: UNIVERSITY PARK PRESS
    300 North Charles Street
    Baltimore, Maryland 21201

ORDER FORM

Please include full
payment or credit card
charge authorization
with this order.

Send me _____ set(s) of **Analysis Forms** for **Ingram: Procedures for the Phonological Analysis of Children's Language** (each set contains: 20 lexicon sheets, 30 consonant inventory sheets, 10 phonological processes sheets, 10 item and replica sheets, 10 child syllable sheets, 10 homonymy sheets) at **$9.95 per set.**

Amount enclosed in full payment of this order _____

Charge this purchase to my ☐ American Express ☐ Master Charge

☐ VISA   Card expiration date_____

Name _____

Address _____

Account No. _____

_____ Zip Code _____

Signature _____

Thank you

Price subject to change without notice. Analysis forms are nonreturnable.

Assessing Communicative Behavior, Volume I

ASSESSING LANGUAGE PRODUCTION IN CHILDREN
EXPERIMENTAL PROCEDURES

by
Jon F. Miller, *Ph.D.*

Professor and Section Head, Communicative Disorders, Waisman Center on Mental Retardation and Human Development, University of Wisconsin-Madison
With chapters by **Thomas M. Klee, M.A.,** and **Rhea Paul, M.A.,** Department of Communicative Disorders, and **Robin S. Chapman, Ph.D.,** Professor of Communicative Disorders, University of Wisconsin-Madison.

Here is the first comprehensive source of informal assessment procedures proven effective under clinical conditions. In this handy, workbook-sized volume a master clinician distills the findings of six years of testing at the Waisman Center on Mental Retardation and Human Development, where theory and research have been applied to the practical problems of developmental assessment. In compiling this outstanding volume, author Jon F. Miller has produced a masterful and important work for every speech and language clinician who deals with developmentally disabled children under the age of eight—an age group especially difficult to test by standardized methods.

Miller's insightful findings confirm that:
- Assessment protocols must be individualized for each child.
- It is often necessary to utilize a variety of methods·to assess a particular behavior.
- Experimental nonstandardized, informal, criterion-referenced procedures are often the best sources of information.

Invaluable in the preparation of IEP's, this book is unexcelled as a reference for procedures, content selection, and interpreting criteria necessary for the informal evaluation of productive language behavior. It is an excellent textbook for advanced undergraduate and masters-level courses in diagnostic procedures and language disorders, as well as in speech and hearing and special education programs, and is a must for every speech-language clinician whose practice includes young children, and for practitioners in special education and educational psychology.

Contents for ASSESSING LANGUAGE PRODUCTION IN CHILDREN

Contributions and procedures by:
Ursula Bellugi
Rhea Paul
Robin S. Chapman
Joe Reichle
Carol Goossens
Susan Schmidt
Ellen Green
Shelley Schwimmer Gluck
Susan Marks
Shelly Werner
Helen Frye-Osier
David E. Yoder

200 pages   *Paperback*   *8½" × 11"*   *Illustrated*   **1981**
ISBN 0-8391-1598-9   *Stock No. 17248*

To order immediately...   **Or write:**

**Call Toll Free
800-638-7511**

**In Maryland call
(301) 547-0700**

UNIVERSITY PARK PRESS
International Publishers in Science, Medicine, and Education
**300 North Charles Street
Baltimore, Maryland 21201**